The Labrador Retriever

OUR BEST FRIENDS

The Boxer
Caring for Your Mutt
The German Shepherd
The Golden Retriever
The Labrador Retriever
The Poodle
The Shih Tzu
The Yorkshire Terrier

OUR BEST FRIENDS

The Labrador Retriever

Sandra Bolan

ELDORADO INK

Produced by OTTN Publishing, Stockton, New Jersey

Eldorado Ink
PO Box 100097
Pittsburgh, PA 15233
www.eldoradoink.com

First printing

1 3 5 7 9 8 6 4 2

Library of Congress Cataloging-in-Publication Data

Bolan, Sandra.
  The Labrador retriever / Sandra Bolan.
    p. cm. — (Our best friends)
  Includes bibliographical references and index.
  ISBN-13: 978-1-932904-23-9 (hc)
  ISBN-10: 1-932904-23-9 (hc)
  1. Labrador retriever—Juvenile literature. I. Title.
  SF429.L3B64 2008
  636.752'7—dc22

                          2007044876

Photo credits: © American Animal Hospital Association: 47; © Sandra Bolan: 51,
97 (both), 106, 109; © Paula Holzapfel: front cover (left top); © iStockphoto.com/
Stacey Bates: 8; © iStockphoto.com/Szelmek: 45; © iStockphoto.com/André Weyer:
69; Courtesy National Association of Professional Pet Sitters, www.petsitters.org:
89; © Will Patch: 55; © Photos.com: 84; used under license from Shutterstock,
Inc.: 3, 10, 11, 13, 15, 16 (dog and flag), 17, 19, 20, 21, 22, 23, 24, 25, 29, 30, 32,
33, 34, 36, 37, 39, 41, 48, 50, 52, 59, 60, 61, 63, 64, 67, 71, 72, 75, 77, 82, 83
(top and bottom), 85, 86, 90, 91, 93, 98, 99, 101, 104, 107, 110, 111, front cover
(main, left center, and left bottom), back cover.

TABLE OF CONTENTS

Introduction by Gary Korsgaard, DVM   6

1   Is a Labrador Retriever Right for You?   9

2   History and Characteristics of the Labrador Retriever   16

3   Know Your Responsibilities   24

4   Getting off on the Right Paw   32

5   What to Expect During the First Six Months   50

6   Your Lab Is Growing Up   77

7   Things to Do With Your Adult Lab   90

8   The Golden Years   104

Organizations to Contact   112

Further Reading   114

Internet Resources   115

Index   116

About the Author   120

Introduction

GARY KORSGAARD, DVM

The mutually beneficial relationship between humans and animals began long before the dawn of recorded history. Archaeologists believe that humans began to capture and tame wild goats, sheep, and pigs more than 9,000 years ago. These animals were then bred for specific purposes, such as providing humans with a reliable source of food or providing furs and hides that could be used for clothing or the construction of dwellings.

Other animals had been sought for companionship and assistance even earlier. The dog, believed to be the first animal domesticated, began living and working with Stone Age humans in Europe more than 14,000 years ago. Some archaeologists believe that wild dogs and humans were drawn together because both hunted the same prey. By taming and training dogs, humans became more effective hunters. Dogs, meanwhile, enjoyed the social contact with humans and benefited from greater access to food and warm shelter. Dogs soon became beloved pets as well as trusted workers. This can be seen from the many artifacts depicting dogs that have been found at ancient sites in Asia, Europe, North America, and the Middle East.

The earliest domestic cats appeared in the Middle East about 5,000 years ago. Small wild cats were probably first attracted to human settlements because plenty of rodents could be found wherever harvested grain was stored. Cats played a useful role in hunting and killing these pests, and it is likely that grateful humans rewarded them for this assistance. Over time, these small cats gave up some of their aggressive wild behaviors and began living among humans. Cats eventually became so popular in ancient Egypt that they were believed to possess magical powers. Cat statues were placed outside homes to ward off evil spirits, and mummified cats were included in royal tombs to accompany their owners into the afterlife.

Today, few people believe that cats have supernatural powers, but most pet owners feel a magical bond with their pets, whether they are dogs, cats, hamsters, rabbits, horses, or parrots. The lives of pets and their people become inextricably intertwined, providing strong emotional and physical rewards for both humans and animals. People of all ages can benefit from the loving companionship of a pet. Not surprisingly, then, pet ownership is widespread. Recent statistics indicate that about 60 percent of all households in the United States and Canada have at least one pet, while the figure is close to 50 percent of households in the United Kingdom. For millions of people, therefore, pets truly have become their "best friends."

Finding the best animal friend can be a challenge, however. Not only are there many types of domesticated pets, but each has specific needs, characteristics, and personality traits. Even within a category of pets, such as dogs, different breeds will flourish in different surroundings and with different treatment. For example, a German Shepherd may not be the right pet for a person living in a cramped urban apartment; that person might be better off caring for a smaller dog like a Toy Poodle or Shih Tzu, or perhaps a cat. On the other hand, an active person who loves the outdoors may prefer the companion-

ship of a Labrador Retriever to that of a small dog or a passive indoor pet like a goldfish or hamster.

The joys of pet ownership come with certain responsibilities. Bringing a pet into your home and your neighborhood obligates you to care for and train the pet properly. For example, a dog must be housebroken, taught to obey your commands, and trained to behave appropriately when he encounters other people or animals. Owners must also be mindful of their pet's particular nutritional and medical needs.

The purpose of the OUR BEST FRIENDS series is to provide a helpful and comprehensive introduction to pet ownership. Each book contains the basic information a prospective pet owner needs in order to choose the right pet for his or her situation and to care for that pet throughout the pet's lifetime. Training, socialization, proper nutrition, potential medical issues, and the legal responsibilities of pet ownership are thoroughly explained and discussed, and an abundance of expert tips and suggestions are offered. Whether it is a hamster, corn snake, guinea pig, or Labrador Retriever, the books in the OUR BEST FRIENDS series provide everything the reader needs to know about how to have a happy, well-adjusted, and well-behaved pet.

The Labrador Retriever's friendly, fun-loving, and loyal disposition makes it a popular pet.

CHAPTER ONE

Is a Labrador Retriever Right for You?

You've decided to become the owner of a Labrador Retriever. Congratulations! You are embarking on years of enjoyment, love, laughter, and companionship that will be accompanied by a few chewed shoes or table legs and cleared counters.

You are not alone in your love for the Lab. Since 1991, the Labrador Retriever has been rated the most popular dog in the United States, according to the American Kennel Club (AKC). The AKC tracks all registered purebred dogs in the United States. There are similar organizations in Canada (the Canadian Kennel Club), and in Britain (the Kennel Club of the United Kingdom). In 2005, the Lab was the most popular dog in all three countries.

What makes the Labrador Retriever so popular? These dogs possess qualities that appeal to virtually everyone: they're playful, hardworking and great with people, including children, which makes them great family dogs. These are also the same qualities that enable the Labrador Retriever to be great service dogs.

Labs are born retrievers, which is why they are also great for the avid hunter. And once the hunt is over, Labs can seamlessly switch gears to become the hunter's loyal companion.

Labs are not, however, for everyone. If you are looking for a guard dog, keep searching. While some

Labs were originally bred to accompany hunters.

people may find the Lab's size somewhat intimidating—they can weigh as much as 80 pounds (36 kg) once fully grown—these dogs are likely to give an initial bark and then lick an intruder, not frighten him away.

Labs are very energetic. After all, they were originally bred to work out in the field all day. So, if reading a good book in front of the fire is your ideal pastime, then a Lab is probably not for you. Labs enjoy snuggling with their human companions—it just takes a lot of runs around the park to get them there.

EASY-GOING TEMPERAMENT

The Lab's easygoing demeanor is another reason for his popularity. A Labrador Retriever loves to please and is not aggressive towards people—friend or foe. And despite their size, Labs are very gentle, albeit a little clumsy.

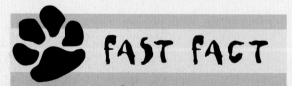

FAST FACT

Before acquiring a Labrador Retriever, be prepared to make a long-term commitment. The lifespan of the average Lab is 13 to 15 years.

Although the Lab is considered one of the smartest dogs around, Labs are slow to mentally mature. Their bodies fully mature around 12 to 18 months of age, like other breeds, but it takes another one to two years for the Lab to intellectually mature, which leaves you with a big puppy on your hands. This delayed onset of adulthood is another wonderful characteristic of the breed—as long as you have a sense of humor, because your Lab will do some really strange things during this time.

A LAB'S ROLE IN YOUR LIFE

Before you bring home your Lab, you have to first decide what his role in your life will be. Will your Lab become a top show dog, companion hunter, field trial champion, or just your constant mate? No matter which one you choose, your Lab will feel right at home and excel at his required tasks, as long as you take the time to train him properly.

Labrador Retrievers make great family pets.

FAST FACT

Labs come in only three colors: black, chocolate and yellow. Yellow Labs come in a variety of shades, however; from almost white to fox-red.

If you want a family pet with a job, but don't hunt or want to participate in fieldwork, there are numerous volunteer organizations that train and work with dogs and their owners; several are listed at the end of this book. This is a terrific way to give your Lab meaningful work to do without a competitive atmosphere.

THE BEST ENVIRONMENT FOR YOUR LAB

You may love the idea of owning a Labrador Retriever, but do you really have what it takes to be his owner and companion for the next 13 to 15 years?

Every year, hundreds of Labs are dropped off at local shelters because owners don't realize how much work these dogs really require. So make sure you are willing to make a lifetime commitment.

It is imperative that your entire family be on board with the decision to bring a dog into the household. Assuming your partner will change his or her mind and fall in love with the dog once he has arrived is not good enough.

Commitment, patience, stubbornness, and sense of humor are all characteristics that not only describe the typical Lab, but also describe the ideal Lab owner. Another quality of a good Lab owner includes being able to be firm but kind, especially when it comes to training. You must clearly indicate what you want from your Lab, and then shower him with praise when he does it. Being too kind and allowing your Lab do whatever he wants when he wants will only cause chaos.

Having an active lifestyle is also imperative, as Labs are high-energy dogs. If a Lab doesn't get enough human-directed exercise, such as long walks, romps in the park, or even obedience training, he will cre-

ate his own activities that will typically consist of chewing your shoes, walls, and furniture.

Labs don't require a lot of grooming—regular brushing (once a week) and an occasional bath (typically around twice a year, if they start to smell unpleasant) will suffice. However, they aren't necessarily the cleanest dogs either. A run through the dog park might result in your yellow Lab coming home looking more black than yellow. But the good news is that with a towel and grooming brush, the dirt will come off quite easily.

You, on the other hand, may need a shower, as Labs love to share their discoveries with everyone. This often means that once your Lab has rolled through a muddy puddle he will come bounding up to you and, in an effort to make himself presentable, give himself a good shake that will send the mud flying onto you. This is where a sense of humor is imperative.

While Labs have short, coarse fur, they are not immune to shedding. These dogs actually shed quite a bit, with the worst of it occurring in the spring when the Lab sheds his thicker, winter coat in favor of a lighter one. Another period of significant shedding occurs again in the fall, in prepara-

If you enjoy an active lifestyle, a Labrador Retriever may be the ideal pet for you. Labs have energy to burn and will take pleasure in your outdoor activities.

tion for the Lab's thicker coat that's required for the colder months.

THE HIGH PRICE OF OWNING A CHEWER

The cost of owning a Lab varies based on a number of factors such as your dog's overall health and age. During a Labrador Retriever's first year you could spend anywhere from $850 to more than $2,000 just for his care, and that does not include the actual price of the dog. The cost of Lab ownership breaks down like this:

ROUTINE VETERINARY CARE: $100 to $500. The price varies so much because it depends on how much your veterinarian charges for examinations and which tests are conducted.

GETTING THE RIGHT STUFF

It is extremely easy to go overboard, spoiling your new Lab with tons of toys and the nicest bed. However, Labs have simple needs—something hard, yet soothing to the gums, to chew on, and a basic dog bed will suffice. (Although, if given the chance, he'll happily sleep on your bed!)

You will want to spend a bit more on his food and water bowls. Buy ceramic or metal bowls—plastic ones are cheaper, but bacteria can build up on plastic and this can lead to upset stomachs. Labs will also chew up plastic bowls, so you are better off investing in a good bowl right from the start.

When it comes to toys, make sure to buy toys that are durable. When looking for chew toys, check the package's chew meter. Labs are strong chewers even as puppies, so pick toys with a high chew threshold. No toy is indestructible, so whenever you give your Lab a new toy, stay with him while he plays with it, especially if you suspect it may not last that long. If it comes apart, take the toy away so your Lab cannot ingest small, sharp pieces.

NON-ROUTINE VETERINARY CARE: It is a good idea to have a slush fund available, just in case, as accidents are bound to happen. The price will vary depending on how many emergency visits have to be made.

PARASITE TREATMENT AND CONTROL: $100 to $150. This is an annual cost, and includes flea and heartworm prevention.

FOOD AND TREATS: $150 to $500. There is a broad price range because it greatly depends on the quality of food you feed your puppy. A premium brand food is preferred; although it costs more, your dog will have an overall healthier life and will require less medical attention. Treats should also be of a very high quality.

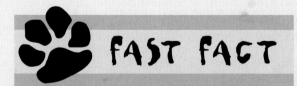

FAST FACT

While it is a good idea to budget for routine vet bills, you may also want to have an emergency fund on hand in case your Lab has an accident or an unexpected illness. Some vets will not allow you to charge visits on a credit card, but instead require cash.

Even as puppies Labs are strong chewers, so be sure to purchase durable toys.

IMMUNIZATION, INCLUDING RABIES: $50 to $100. This is an expense that you should expect on an annual basis.

SPAYING OR NEUTERING: $50 to $200. This is a one-time fee. Again, the price varies depending on what your vet charges.

MISCELLANEOUS EXPENSES: $200 to $2,000. This includes toys, collars, leashes, bowls, and grooming supplies (see sidebar, page 14).

EQUIPMENT: $100. This includes a crate and baby gates, both of which are an absolute must when it comes to house training.

OBEDIENCE SCHOOL: $100 to $500. You don't need to spend a fortune on obedience training, but you must choose a school that is right for you. Classes held in a pet store cost about $100 per session. Training classes held in other locations can cost upwards of $200 to $300 a session. Another option is private training, which costs about $50/hour. If you decide to participate in an activity like agility, the cost of training will increase further.

CHAPTER TWO

History and Characteristics of the Labrador Retriever

With the name "Labrador Retriever," it's logical to conclude that this breed of dog originated from Labrador, a region in Eastern Canada. But that's actually not quite the case. Newfoundland, an island in Eastern Canada, is the actual birthplace of the Labrador Retriever. (Today, Newfoundland is part of a Canadian province that includes Labrador.)

It is believed that European fishermen and hunters who came to Eastern Canada during the 16th and 17th centuries brought with them dogs that resembled the Lab to help them retrieve fish from the icy waters or find fallen fowl on land. The ancestors of the Lab include dogs native to the region (possibly introduced by the Vikings hundreds of years earlier), as well as the St. Hubert hound of France, Portuguese

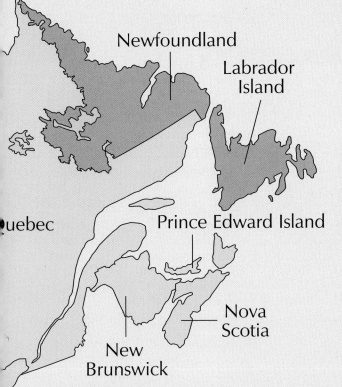

The Labrador Retriever breed was developed in Newfoundland, a province in eastern Canada.

mastiffs, and various European pointer breeds. Through years of selective breeding, two distinct lines of dogs emerged—the large, long-haired Newfoundland and the Labrador Retriever.

It was the Lab that became the fisherman's working dog of choice because his size and coat was more suitable to the required tasks. Labs were small enough to fit into the two-man shallow-draft dories used by the fishermen to tend their offshore nets. Labs are good swimmers, and could be trained to help pull a net to shore.

Labs returned to Europe in the late 18th century to become hunting companions for wealthy English landowners. Over time, word of the Lab's exceptional hunting ability spread from England's aristocracy to sportsmen throughout the country, increasing the demand for these hard-working dogs.

Labrador Retrievers were slower to gain acceptance in the United States. The American Kennel Club officially recognized the breed in 1917, but ten years later there were only 23 registered Labs in the country. However, an article the next year in the AKC publication *American Kennel Gazette* brought the breed greater attention. In 1931 the Labrador Retriever Club was formed in the United States.

The popularity of Labrador Retrievers continued to grow over the next six decades, particularly in the years after World War II. In

For hunters and settlers, the soft mouth of the Lab was imperative, as they needed the Lab to bring their fallen fowl or fish back to them in one piece.

EARLY BREEDERS

The most eminent English breeder of Labrador Retrievers in the 19th century was the third Earl of Malmesbury. He imported specially selected Labs and St. John's Dogs from Newfoundland for breeding purposes. Malmesbury is credited with setting the Labrador Retriever breed standard. Other 19th century English aristocrats who were prominent breeders included the fifth Duke of Buccleugh; his brother, Lord John Scott; and the twelfth Earl of Home.

In 1885, however, two pieces of legislation threatened the future of the Labrador breed. In England, the Quarantine Act prevented dogs and other livestock from being imported to the island for six months. In Canada, the Newfoundland Sheep Protection Act enabled regions to charge for dog licenses. This piece of legislation caused many Lab owners to destroy dogs they didn't use for working purposes, because it became too costly to keep them.

The two laws led to a drastic decline in the number of Labs being shipped to England for breeding purposes. This forced Lab breeders like Malmesbury, Buccleugh, and Home to perfect the breed through careful reproduction of their available stock. Although the St. John's breed died out, the Labrador Retriever thrived.

1991, the Labrador Retriever became the most popular dog registered by the American Kennel Club—a status the breed retains to this day.

WHY THE LAB IS BELOVED

All of the tasks initially required of the Labrador Retriever have made him the dog he is today—people oriented, water loving, and hard-working.

CONSTANT COMPANION: Labs initially not only worked alongside their owners, they also became the family companion. The result? People-oriented dogs capable of working hard all day—on land or in water—then coming home and hanging out with their owner by the fire.

INDEPENDENT: Early Labs had to willingly leave their owner's side in order to complete their work. This resulted in the independent Lab of today, which is capable of being left alone, provided he has a task to occupy his time.

MISCHIEF-MAKER: Today's Labs have a relatively short attention span, but that is not because they are unintelligent—it's because they have a very low tolerance for boredom. These dogs were bred to work hard and often. But for the most part, Labs today don't have to work particularly hard, so they become bored. Being the clever, resourceful dogs they are, a bored Lab is a troublemaking Lab. He will discover ways to clear a counter, jump a fence, or escape from a crate.

RETRIEVER: Labs were originally bred to catch fish or retrieve fallen fowl. Although today's Labs are often bred for showing or hunting, they are born retrievers and, given the chance, will gladly fetch your slippers or the newspaper.

BREED STANDARDS AND CONFORMATION

According to the American Kennel Club, which is the breed standard authority for dogs in the United States, the Labrador Retriever is a "strongly built, medium-sized, short-coupled dog possessing sound, athletic, well-balanced conformation that enables it to function as a retrieving gun dog; the substance and soundness to hunt waterfowl or upland game for long hours under difficult conditions; the character and quality to win in the show ring; and the temperament to be a family companion.

"Physical features and mental characteristics should denote a dog bred to perform as an efficient retriever of game with stable temperament suitable for a variety of pursuits beyond the hunting environment."[1]

If a dog fails to meet the AKC's standards, then it is not eligible to participate in AKC-sanctioned events or competitions. This does not, however, mean that he cannot be a great family dog. It just means

Labs can be trained to retrieve things other than prey—including your newspaper.

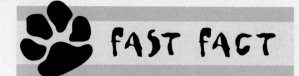

that he cannot be shown or field tried competitively.

SIZE: A male Lab over the age of 12 months must be 22 to 24 inches (56 to 61 cm) in height at the withers (shoulders), according to the AKC. A female Lab that is at least 12 months old should measure 21 to 23 inches (53 to 58 cm) in height. A one-inch variance up or down is allowed, according to the AKC's breed standard.

Males in working condition must weigh between 65 and 80 pounds (29 and 36 kg), while females are to be between 55 and 70 pounds (25 and 32 kg).

STRUCTURE: Dogs must be properly proportioned, which means a male or female Lab should be as long (shoulders to bum) as tall; the Lab's elbows must be located halfway between the ground and withers; and the Lab's chest should go down to the elbows. A long and low, or tall and leggy, Lab is deemed to be disproportioned and not up to AKC standards.

The dog's bone structure must also be in proportion to his or her size—being too light or too heavy boned is unacceptable, according to the AKC.

The dewclaws, located on the upper part of the front paws, may or may not be removed—either is acceptable to the American Kennel Club.

NOSE: A yellow or black Lab's nose is supposed to be black, while chocolate Labs have brown noses. Color fading is not considered a fault, but a completely pink nose or one without any pigmentation is

If you're looking for a show dog, keep the breed standard in mind. But many dogs that would be disqualified from shows—such as this pink-nosed Lab—still make great pets.

A Lab that meets the breed standard has the build and characteristics of a hunting dog.

cause for disqualification, according to the breed standard.

TEETH: A level bite is acceptable, but the preferred normal bite enables the lower teeth to sit just behind and touch the inside of the upper incisors. The AKC deems an underbite or overbite to be a fault.

EARS: A Lab's ears should be set relatively far back on its head, low on the skull and slightly above eye level. They must also be proportionate to the skull.

EYES: Yellow and black Labs have brown eyes with black rims, whereas chocolate Labs have brown or hazel eyes and brown rims. A lack of rim pigmentation is an AKC fault. The eyes of a purebred

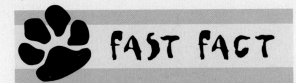

FAST FACT

The Kennel Club of the United Kingdom recognized Labrador Retrievers as an official breed in 1903.

Labrador Retriever are commonly described as friendly, alert, and intelligent.

TAIL: A Lab's tail is unique in that it is thick at the base and thinner at the tip (it has been described as being "otter-like"). The tail is medium in length and should extend no longer than to the dog's hock and have a rounded appearance. The tail should also be straight and not curl over the dog's rear. Docking or bobbing of the tail—cutting off part or all of it—is grounds for disqualification in AKC Conformation competitions.

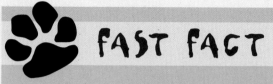

FAST FACT

The first U.S. field trial for Labs was held in Chester, New York, in 1931.

COLOR AND COAT: The Labrador Retriever comes in three colors— yellow, black, and chocolate. Black Labs are pure black with no other color markings on their bodies. Chocolate and yellow Labs, however, can vary in shade: from light to dark chocolate Labs, or from fox-red to almost-white yellow Labs. All of

According to the breed standard, there are three acceptable colors for Labrador Retrievers (left to right): yellow, chocolate, and black.

While the Lab's outermost coat is coarse enough to repel most dirt and mud, sometimes he will need a good soapy bath.

these variations are acceptable within the AKC breed standard.

You may hear of "silver Labs," which have a coat that is silvery or a light chocolate. However, silver Labs are not purebreds, and neither the American Kennel Club nor the Labrador Retriever Club officially recognizes the color. Silver Labs are usually produced by disreputable backyard breeders and should be avoided.

The Lab has what is known as a double coat. The soft and downy undercoat keeps the dog warm and dry in cold weather, while the coarse, water-repellent outer coat repels water and most dirt. This makes the Lab's coat easy to clean—just rub a hand or towel over the dirt and it will fall off.

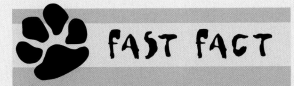

FAST FACT

The St. John's Dog, a Canadian ancestor of the Labrador Retriever, became extinct in the late 19th century.

CHAPTER THREE

Know Your Responsibilities

Owning a dog comes with a lot of responsibilities. Not only do you have to feed him and ensure he remains in good health, you also have to provide your Lab with an ample amount of exercise and mental stimulation, as they are very active and smart—and, when not given enough direction, destructive.

Your house, including the backyard, has to be suitable for your Lab. There has to be a solid and high fence surrounding your yard, and there cannot be any holes in the fence. The gate must also have a secure lock.

Not only does your dog need to have manners when he is in the

If you plan to let your Lab roam the backyard, make sure that your fence is at least six feet tall and that there is no easy way for him to get underneath it.

house, he also has to have them while in the backyard and when out walking around the neighborhood. If your dog is a chronic barker, you must immediately bring him into the house so you don't anger your neighbors.

When out for a walk with your dog, he must be on a leash unless you are in a designated leash-free zone. When in a leash-free park, follow the rules, which will include picking up after him. You must also pick up after him when he does his business while on your walk.

IDENTIFICATION

Every year, thousands of dogs are either stolen or lost, which is why it is imperative that your dog have some form of identification.

A collar with your dog's name and a phone number is a good idea, but refrain from putting your address on the tag. An unscrupulous

It is always a good idea to keep your Labrador Retriever on a leash when you're out in public areas.

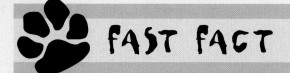

FAST FACT

person can easily befriend your Lab, then use their friendly encounter to his advantage when he breaks into your home. Remember, Labs make lousy guard dogs.

You may want to put something like "requires medication" on the tag, along with a phone number, so the person who finds your dog contacts you immediately.

Collars and tags have a bad habit of falling off, and they can be easily taken off, so ideally your pet should be identifiable by a more permanent means.

One type of permanent identification is a tattoo. Dogs can be tattooed either inside an ear or on the inside of a thigh. Each dog gets a unique number, which is then registered, along with your contact information, with a pet recovery organization like the National Dog Registry. Tattooing can be done at any time during a dog's life, but the breeder will often

do this in the very early weeks of his life. One downside is that, if the dog is tattooed when he is very young, the tattoo will become unreadable as he grows and may have to be redone.

Another form of permanent identification is a tiny microchip, which is injected deep between the dog's shoulder blades via a needle. This is done by a veterinarian trained in the process, and is no more painful to your Lab than a regular vaccine injection. Over time, a layer of connective tissue grows around the chip, which prevents it from moving around in the dog's body. The chip is made of material that will not cause any adverse effects in your dog. Each chip includes a unique number. If your Lab does become lost, and is brought to a veterinarian clinic or shelter anywhere in North America, the staff can scan the dog's back with a special microchip reader to find the owner. Your contact information will come up and you will be contacted and reunited with your dog.

THE GREAT SPAY/NEUTER DEBATE

Unless you intend to show your Lab in Conformation shows, enter him into professional field trials, or use him as breed stock, consider spaying or neutering your Lab. This will not only prevent any unplanned puppies, it is also better for your dog's health and will make your Lab a more well-behaved and easier dog to live with.

Spaying (removing the female's reproductive organs) reduces a female Lab's chances of suffering from potentially fatal conditions such as ovarian and uterine cancer, or from pyometra, a potentially lethal uterine infection. It also reduces her chances of suffering from mammary tumors. In addition, spaying will make it easier to care for your female Lab. An intact female has two heat cycles a year (every six to nine months, on average), and during these times she discharges blood for about a month. Spaying your Lab enables you to avoid this messy situation.

Neutering a male Lab (removing his testicles) will reduce his drive to roam. An intact male can smell an intact female from miles away and will do whatever he can to reach her. That includes digging under fences and crossing busy streets, regardless of potential injury. A neutered male, on the other hand, is less likely to roam, and also will be less inclined to mount anything and everything (including visitors' legs) or mark everywhere he goes with urine. Neutering will also curtail his aggression towards other dogs, which is important if you live in a multi-dog house or if you plan to put your Lab in doggie day care.

Dogs should be spayed or neutered when they are between the ages of six and 12 months old. If possible, a female should be spayed before her first heat cycle.

Spaying and neutering is somewhat controversial among dog owners. Some people refuse to spay or neuter their pets because they have heard stories about negative side effects. These stories are largely untrue. One common myth is that a dog's personality will change—your happy, spunky Lab will become disinterested in all fun things. Another myth is that a spayed or neutered Lab will become fat and lazy. Neither of those things will occur. Your Lab may become more interested in food, but you just need to keep him active and cut back on the cookies.

Some people don't think they can afford to spay or neuter their dog. However, many veterinary clinics will make payment arrangements for people with financial constraints in order to help keep Labs in good

FAST FACT

Always remember to pick up solid waste after your dog does his business when he is out in public. The fines can be pretty hefty for leaving it behind.

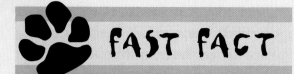

health. Some local shelters offer discounted prices for spaying or neutering, whether you adopted your Lab from the shelter or from a breeder.

PET INSURANCE

Pet insurance has been available for more than 20 years, but only in the past few years have people been purchasing it for their dogs. Dog owners purchase pet insurance for peace of mind. For a minimal amount of money each month, you know that if anything serious (an accident or cancer, for example) happens to your Lab, you will be able to afford his treatment. Pet insurance means that you don't have to make the difficult decision between treating your dog and putting him down because the treatment is too expensive.

Labs are active dogs and, depending on how vigorous your activities with him are, you may decide that insuring him right from the start is a good idea. People who prefer to participate in less-intense activities with their Labs may opt to forgo pet insurance altogether or wait until their Lab is older, when many health problems start to occur.

Situations typically covered by pet insurance policies include:
- accidental damage caused by the dog

DOGS AS PROPERTY

Dogs are legally defined as property, which means they have no rights. However, in some parts of the United States, the legal status of dogs is slowly changing. Several cities, along with the state of Rhode Island, now refer to pet owners as guardians and to dogs as companions, not property. Supporters of this change say it will allow the legal system to impose greater penalties against people who abuse or neglect their dogs.

- illness
- third-party liability
- legal expenses
- emergency boarding fees
- vacation cancellation due to your dog becoming ill or injured.

For the most part, elective procedures such as teeth cleaning or spaying or neutering are not covered by insurance policies. Annual vet visits and vaccinations are also not normally covered. Preexisting medical conditions are often excluded, as are diseases certain breeds are prone to, such as hip dysplasia for Labs.

Like car and home insurance, your coverage, deductibles, and rates will vary by company. Before you purchase pet insurance, do some homework.

THE LAW AND YOUR LAB

Your municipality probably requires dogs to be registered with the local animal officer. The fee, if applicable, will depend on where you live. Many cities offer discounted licensing fees to dogs that have been spayed or neutered. Additional discounts may also be given for dogs that have a permanent form of identification, such as a tattoo or microchip.

Be respectful of your neighbors. Keeping your Lab from barking excessively is not only considerate, but also required by law in many communities.

Like any dog, a Labrador Retriever is capable of aggressive behavior. It's important to train your dog well and keep him under control at all times.

You also need to know whether your municipality or state has a law regarding noises your dog makes. Specific laws regarding excessive barking are relatively rare, but often barking will fall under the general nuisance or noise bylaws. This puts the onus on the dog owner to keep pets quiet. For example, the local ordinance may prohibit loud or excessive noise after 11 P.M. If neighbors continually complain to the police about a barking dog, and the owner fails to do anything despite the repeated warnings, the owner may be fined or arrested for disturbing the peace.

Perhaps the most common reason for a dog owner to become entangled in the legal system comes as a result of his pet biting another dog or person. According to the Center for Disease Control in Atlanta, dogs bite about 4.7 million people in the United States every year. Of those bite victims, 800,000 require some form of medical attention.

As the Lab's owner, you are responsible for his actions, as well as for paying the resulting medical costs, which—depending on the severity of the bite and the litigious-ness of the victim—can be enormous. The best way to avoid this situation is to ensure your Lab never has the opportunity to cause anyone any harm. This is accomplished through proper training, as well as by having care and control of your Lab at all times, including when you are away from home or when he is in the care of other people.

In order to avoid getting involved in a situation where a child is bitten by your dog, despite him being secured in the backyard, post signs such as "No Trespassing" and "Beware of Dog."

Thankfully, Labs are good-natured and biting is usually not a problem. However, Labs are capable of aggressive behavior at any time, no matter how well trained, so their owners must always be vigilant.

HEY! NO BITING!

Following are some tips to prevent your Lab from being accused of biting a person or another dog:

- train and socialize him
- never let him off his leash unless in a designated off-leash area
- watch your Lab carefully, especially when he is around children

- if a stranger approaches while you and your pet are walk-ing, move out of his way, especially if your dog starts to get his hackles up
- post warning signs on your property to keep strangers from approaching your Lab

CHAPTER FOUR

Getting off on the Right Paw

You've done your research, evaluated your lifestyle, and concluded that you and your children would enjoy having an exuberant and large dog in your life. You've also taken into consideration your other pets. Labs are great with other dogs, cats, or even pocket pets, especially when they are trained to look and not touch. Cats may get their noses out of joint, but that's also part and parcel of their personality. The cat will let your Lab know who the boss is. If you already have a dog in your home, you need to be confident that he or she will welcome the new Lab into the family.

A Labrador Retriever can coexist with your other pets—even cats.

Your next step is to decide on your new dog's role within the household. Will he be the family pet, show dog, sporting dog, or all of the above? You also have to decide if you want a male or female Lab, and whether you want a puppy—with all that entails—or if an older dog is more suitable.

KNOW WHAT YOU WANT

In order to properly choose your Lab, you need to know if you want to show your dog, compete with him in field trials, or just want a house pet. Keep in mind that a show or field dog will also make a great family pet, but a Lab bred for show purposes may not necessarily be a great field dog, and vice versa.

Right now, you're asking yourself: is there really a difference between show and sport Labs? The answer is yes. A dog's lineage very much dictates a puppy's bone structure, temperament, and skill set. Structurally, show dogs are short and stocky with a broad head. A show Lab generally has a laid-back personality. These Labs have not lost their ability to retrieve—or get into typical Lab trouble—they have just been bred for a less-vigorous lifestyle.

A field Lab looks very different than one bred for the show ring. Field Labs have a leaner body, longer legs, and a narrower head. All of these attributes help make the dog's day out in the field a bit easier on his body.

If you want to show your dog, as well as compete in field trials and hunt tests, then you should consider getting a show dog. These dogs will be able to compete both in the ring and out in the field. If all you want is a companion dog, then consider choosing a puppy with show-ring

Your lifestyle, and your expectations for your Labrador Retriever, will determine whether a puppy or an adult dog is right for you.

lineage. Your Lab will be a little more laid-back compared to the high-energy field Lab, but he will still have tons of energy and will be interested in playing with the kids all day long.

Another question is whether to get a puppy or an adult Lab. Puppies have a way of stealing peoples' hearts, but they are also a lot of work. Adult dogs, on the other hand, come housebroken and, in some cases, obedience trained. This makes the upheaval in your life minimal when compared to caring for a puppy.

In deciding between a puppy and an adult dog, consider your lifestyle. Then discuss with your family the pros and cons of bringing one or the other into your life.

PROS AND CONS OF GETTING A PUPPY

A puppy is cute and adorable, but also frustrating and destructive. When you bring an eight-week-old puppy home, he is a clean slate. He has no idea what "going potty" in the backyard is all about, and he definitely doesn't understand why he can't chew the furniture.

Throughout your day, you will have to watch every move he makes, redirecting him away from the bad behaviors—like pooping in the middle of the living room carpet—and showing him the correct action. You will need to feed him frequently (three to four times a day), and make sure he gets plenty of exercise to help burn off his abundant energy.

But raising a puppy has an upside—it enables you to mold him into the adult dog you want. Keep in mind, though, that you may have to sacrifice a carpet, couch, or shoe along the way.

It is not realistic to expect the owners of a new puppy to stay home with him for the first few months of his life. But even if both owners work, that does not mean they can't manage a puppy. They will just need to get some help.

If you are not able to come home once or twice a day to let your puppy out, feed him, and exercise him, there are numerous options available. You can hire

Labrador puppies are extremely cute, even when they are chewing apart your furniture or otherwise getting into trouble.

a professional pet sitter or ask a dog-loving neighbor to come to your house at specific times throughout the day to do the same thing. Or if one of your children is old enough to take on this responsibility during her school's lunch break, she can come home and give your puppy the care he needs.

PROS AND CONS OF AN ADULT DOG

An adult Lab provides very few surprises, as you will already know his full-grown size, conformation, and temperament. Knowing these things is particularly beneficial if you are interested in getting a show or field dog, or if you know for sure that a puppy is not the best choice for you.

Depending on your lifestyle, an older Labrador may be more appropriate than a puppy because he is content to sleep all day when no one is home, instead of tearing things up because there is no one around to stop him. Keep in mind, though, that you must provide your adult Lab with lots of mentally and physically stimulating activities. This is something you will never be able to avoid, no matter how old your Lab is.

If you have children in the house, try to find out whether the adult Lab has ever lived in a house with chil-dren. Labs have a very gentle nature, which is why they are members of so many families, but if he has never been around a young child before, you may want the two of them to meet before making your final decision. If the Lab has never had his tail pulled by a child, it's going to take him a bit of time to get used to it, but he will.

You also need to consider your other pets. Labs get along with other dogs and even cats, but when you make that initial introduction, especially with another dog, you want to do it on neutral ground so no territorial issues arise with either dog. You also want to make sure both of them are leashed. Chances are they will get along, but just like people, some dogs do not mix.

If the cost of owning a dog is a concern for you, adult Labs cost a bit less in terms of veterinary care because they have already had all of their initial vaccinations and are probably already spayed or neutered. As long as he is in good health, you need only pay for his annual vaccines.

MALE OR FEMALE?

When it comes to personality and temperament, there is a difference between male and female Labrador Retrievers. One gender is not better than the other; they are just different.

The female Labrador Retriever is more popular than the male, probably because of her reputation for being more relaxed. She also won't lift her leg throughout the house to mark her territory. But although female Labs tend to be more laid-back, they can also be very independent and bossy. She also has a reputation for being protective, which includes barking at every strange sound she hears. If you have young children, they will provide the perfect opportunity for your female Lab to use her "mothering" skills.

A female Lab can be affectionate, but only when she wants to be, not necessarily when you want her to be. Much like a cat, she will come up to you, demand to be petted, and get up and leave once she's had enough. She won't necessarily defy your commands, but she will act manipulatively in order to get you to let her do what she wants.

Mood swings are also a part of the female Lab's personality. She can be as sweet as pie one minute, grumpy and sulking in a corner the next. This can be somewhat

Both male (lying down) and female (sitting up) Labs make great pets.

Labs can live with other dogs, as long as their owners make an effort to get them properly acquainted with each other.

neutralized by having her spayed. If you do not spay your female Lab, she will go into heat, or season, twice a year for roughly three weeks each time. During these cycles, she will constantly lick her swollen genitals as well as mount people's legs, or anything else she can find, which can be quite embarrassing when she does it in front of company. This is also a messy phase, as she also discharges blood, which can be light or heavy. You will want to protect your furniture and carpet.

If you want a dog that is very affectionate and has no trouble showing it, then the male Lab is for you. They have often been compared to

Velcro, as a male Lab will sit under your office chair or in your lap, given the chance, even when he is fully grown. Male Labs love the ladies—they're often called "mama's boys" and will stay close to the woman of the household. The male Lab also has a relatively even temperament when compared to a female Lab.

On the downside, males love to challenge their owners for the position of top dog, especially during their teenage phase (six months to two years of age). In addition, male Labs seem clumsier and more child-like than females.

You should also be aware that while Labs, male or female, typically get along with other dogs, a male Lab can become aggressive or try to dominate other male dogs. This does not mean two male dogs cannot live in the same house together—they most definitely can. There just may be a few wrestling matches between the two along the way to determine which is the top dog.

CHOOSING THE RIGHT BREEDER

Once you've decided what kind of Labrador Retriever you want, you need to find the best breeder. Anyone can mate two Labs and sell the puppies, claiming they are pure-breds. But it takes a reputable breeder to mate two healthy Labrador Retrievers in order for the offspring to also be healthy.

So what is a reputable breeder? She is someone more interested in improving the integrity of the breed than making a lot of money quickly. A reputable breeder will have been around dogs—preferably Labs—for a very long time, either by showing them, competing in field trials or hunt tests, or by training them for obedience trials.

A reputable breeder will do genetic testing on the parents in an effort to lower the chances of the puppies being born with hereditary diseases. She will also screen all potential buyers to ensure her puppies go to the best homes. The breeder may require buyers to sign a contract that, among other things, stipulates that their puppy be spayed or neutered by a specific age (usually by the time the puppy is 12 months old). A responsible breeder will also take any of her dogs back at any time, for any reason, should the owner's circumstances become such that he or she is no longer able to properly care for the dog. A good breeder will also never pressure a prospective owner into buying a puppy.

The first place to look for a breeder is the Labrador Retriever Club (LRC). The LRC is sanctioned by the American Kennel Club and is dedicated to preserving the integrity of the breed. You can also do an Internet search for breeders. But make sure any breeder you consider is registered with the AKC, the Canadian Kennel Club, or the Kennel Club of the United Kingdom.

Choose a breeder who produces the type of dog you are looking for—show, field, or companion. Look for

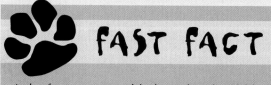

FAST FACT

Labs from a reputable breeder should be able to shine in the show ring, win field trials, or be a great companion dog.

breeders in your geographical area— you don't want to have to drive more than a couple of hours when you're bringing home your new dog. If you and your chosen breeder live in the same area, she may be able to personally help you train your dog for the field or show ring. If she offers a boarding service, this is the ideal place for your Lab when you go away. You will have peace of mind knowing that your Lab is being given the best care possible when you are

not around, and he will appreciate staying in a familiar location.

Once you've identified a few breeders who might be appropriate, call each one and ask about the breeding process and about their facility. A responsible breeder will gladly answer any of your questions, and will probably ask you just as many.

VISITING THE BREEDER

Once you've narrowed down your choices, make arrangements to visit

Good breeders will be happy to introduce you to the mother Lab, although you may not be allowed near her puppies until their immune systems have developed.

the breeders at the top of your list. A reputable breeder will gladly show you around. The purpose of this visit is to look at how the dogs are housed, meet the puppies' parents, and if possible, view the puppies. Not all breeders will let prospective owners meet the puppies prior to the pick-up date. However, some breeders allow the owners to come for a visit once the puppies are five weeks old. At this age, their immune systems are strong enough for cuddling from outsiders.

Any dog you approach—except the new mom, who will be protective of her babies—should be approachable and non-aggressive. Even a new mom shouldn't be particularly aggressive.

QUESTIONS TO ASK POTENTIAL BREEDERS

How long have you been involved with Labs, including breeding?

With how many breeds do you work? *The better breeders will focus on one or two breeds only.*

What titles (in obedience, conformation, hunting, or agility) do the puppies' parents have? *A Lab used for breeding should have titles or be working towards them.*

How were the parents chosen?

Can you provide photos of the parents and other relatives?

What are the ages of the parents? *They need to be at least two years old in order to receive OFA/PenHIP/Wind-Morgan (hip dysplasia) clearance, CERF certificates (eyes), as well as OFA certification.*

Can you provide OFA/PenHIP/Wind-Morgan, CERF, and OFA certificates for both parents?

What vaccines do you give your puppies before they go to their new homes?

At what age can puppies go to their new homes? *This should occur no earlier than seven weeks of age. Puppies need to remain together, and with their mother, for the first seven weeks of their life so they can become properly socialized. Taking a puppy away from his littermates and mother too early can stunt a puppy's emotional development.*

Do you have references? *Get references from people who previously purchased puppies from her. They will give you the most honest reference as they are just like you—new owners of a Lab puppy.*

The average litter has between five and eight puppies. If you're getting your pet from a reputable breeder, she will be able to help you choose the right one.

You may see a lot of dogs on the property—that's okay. What you don't want to see is kennel upon kennel of puppies. A good breeder will only have one or two litters at any one time, and you will likely find them living in the house with the mother dog and the breeder. This is ideal, as it socializes the puppy right from the beginning.

While it may be tempting to take a puppy home right then and there, don't. Take your time in making the final decision about the breeder and her puppies before even thinking about taking one home. Once you've chosen your breeder, let her know right away so you can be placed on the waiting list, if puppies are currently not available.

When you are ready to buy a puppy, a breeder will probably require you to put down a deposit. The amount depends on the cost of the puppy, but it is generally no more than half of the total price.

THE PERFECT PUPPY

Once you've chosen a breeder, you're ready to pick a puppy. But with so many Labs to choose from—an average litter has five to eight puppies—how do you know you're choosing the right one for your family?

Often, the breeder will choose a puppy for you. The breeder will have listened to what you want from your puppy over the long term, and she's spent the last eight weeks watching the puppies' personalities develop. These insights will enable the breeder to match you with the correct pup.

For example, let's say you are a first-time dog owner with a small child. An overly active puppy may not be the ideal choice, as he will run you ragged. But one of the more easygoing, laid-back puppies may be perfect—he will be able to keep up with your young child, but not keep going once everyone is exhausted.

If your breeder allows you to choose your puppy, make sure to ask her about the personality and temperament of each puppy you are considering. She will give you an honest opinion as to whether or not she thinks a particular puppy is a good match with you.

Don't be offended if she suggests a puppy that you hadn't even considered for yourself. Remember, she knows her Labs and the type of person it takes to deal with some of their personality quirks.

PUPPY TESTS

There are a series of puppy tests you can easily do, which will help in making your final decision. You will want to do these simple tests in an area away from the other puppies,

and with the permission of the breeder.

Your ideal puppy should not be too dominant or too submissive, but somewhere in the middle. A puppy (male or female) that is too dominant will generally challenge other dogs and their owners for top billing in the household. You are supposed to be your pet's "pack leader," so unless you are an experienced dog owner it is best to avoid the alpha dog.

On the other hand, a submissive puppy can be just as challenging to live with, as he may start to bite people out of fear. These dogs must be carefully trained and socialized, which is probably too much for the novice dog owner.

FAST FACT

On average, a puppy from a reputable breeder will cost from $500 to $800. An adult Lab, however, can cost anywhere from $100 to $800—it all depends on where you get him. Shelters and rescue organizations generally charge less, but will gladly take more, as donations are the only way they are able to care for these dogs. Breeders traditionally charge the same amount for older Labs as they do for their puppies.

The most respected test is the Volhard Puppy Aptitude Test (PAT) that was developed by world-renowned dog specialists Joachim and Wendy Volhard. The Volhard PAT tests the following characteristics: social attraction, following, restraint, social dominance, and elevation dominance. Scores range from one to six, with three being ideal. A puppy that scores threes, according to the Volhard PAT, "accepts human leaders easily." The test's description goes on to note that a puppy with a score of three is the "best prospect for the average owner, adapts well to new situations and [is] generally good with children and elderly, although it may be inclined to be active. [This dog] makes a good obedience prospect and usually has a common sense approach to life."

The test can be viewed at www.volhard.com/puppy/pat.htm. Score results are interpreted at www.workingdogs.com/testing_volhard.htm.

SOCIAL ATTRACTION: You are testing the puppy's confidence and dependence. Kneel down and clap your hands to get the puppy's attention and coax him towards you. Ideally, the puppy happily comes to you with his tail up.

FOLLOWING: This tests his independence. A puppy that will not follow you is an independent, free-spirited dog that may become difficult to train because he is more interested in the world around him than in you.

You perform the test by simply standing up and walking away from the puppy. Make sure he sees you walk away. The ideal reaction of the puppy will be that he readily follows you with his tail up.

RESTRAINT: This tells us how the puppy accepts stress when he is either physically or socially dominated. In a nutshell, you want to know if he is submissive or dominant.

Gently roll the puppy onto his back and hold him there for 30 seconds. His ideal reaction will be to settle, struggle, then settle again with some eye contact.

SOCIAL DOMINANCE: With the puppy standing and you crouching beside him, pet the puppy from his head to his rump.

The purpose of this test is to see if he will try to dominate you (jump up or nip you), and then walk away. Both reactions indicate an independent dog. You ideally want the puppy to cuddle and lick your face.

ELEVATION DOMINANCE: This is where you test the puppy's ability to accept being dominated in a situation where he has absolutely no control.

Cradle the puppy under his tummy, palms facing upwards and fingers clasped together. Lift the puppy off the ground, but just a little bit. Hold him in the air for 30 seconds.

Ideally, the puppy will not struggle and will relax.

ADOPTION

Breeders are not the only source of great Labs. There are, unfortunately, far too many Labs in shelters or available through rescue organizations.

Puppies are sometimes available from shelters and rescue organizations, but for the most part, Labs

You can test the puppy's retrieval ability, which determines the degree to which the puppy is willing to work with people. This test is imperative for people looking for a field dog or one that will participate in obedience trials. This test has also been used to screen potential guide dogs. When you toss a ball or object, the ideal reaction of the puppy will be that he runs to retrieve it and then returns it to the person who threw the object.

available at these places are male and between the ages of six and 12 months old.

There is nothing wrong with these dogs. These Labs, more often than not, were not purchased from a reputable breeder, but from someone who bred the Labs to make some money. The people who purchased these Labs did not educate themselves about the breed, and when things got tough they just gave up on the dog and brought him to the shelter. Typically, these owners didn't put forth the necessary effort that turns a rambunctious Lab puppy into a well-mannered adult dog.

Other reasons a Lab may end up in a shelter is because the owner's lifestyle has changed (marriage, divorce, new baby); the owner died; or the owner could no longer afford to keep the dog.

Adopting from a shelter or rescue group is not as simple as walking into the shelter, picking a dog and going home with him. Like a breeder, the adoption agency will question you about your lifestyle and reasons for wanting a Lab. They will also ask you about your housing situation—do you rent a home or apartment, or own a home? Do you have a fenced-in backyard? After all, yours is at least the second home this Lab will go to, and these

It's a misconception that adult Labs without permanent homes were all given away because of behavioral problems. You can find some great Labs in animal shelters or through rescue organizations.

organizations want to make sure that it will be his last.

You will be required to complete an adoption application, and may be asked to provide references. If you previously owned a dog, ask your veterinarian or dog trainer to vouch for you. The screening process may also include a home visit prior to adoption. This is to ensure your home is indeed suitable for a Labrador Retriever. Another home visit may occur sometime following the adoption, to confirm that things are going well for you and your new Lab.

The adoption process can be a lengthy one, as it will depend on the number of available dogs, your compatibility with them, and the number of people also wanting to adopt. Sometimes, more than one family will be interested in the same dog. The shelter or rescue organization will make the final decision on who gets the Lab, based on what they observe during the screening process. Do not get discouraged if you don't get the first Lab you try to adopt. Your perfect match will eventually be found.

ADVANTAGES AND DISADVANTAGES TO ADOPTION

There are several advantages to adopting a dog from a shelter. A rescued Labrador Retriever will leave the shelter spayed or neutered and vaccinated. Your new Lab will also have been examined by a veterinarian and marked with some kind of permanent identification tag. Also, you can feel good that you've given a Lab a second chance in a good home

There are, however, some drawbacks to adopting a Lab from a shelter or rescue organization. It can be virtually impossible to tell what the Lab's life was like prior to his surrender, and it is unlikely that anyone at the shelter will know anything about the dog's lineage. More than 50 percent of surrendered Labs are not high-quality purebreds, and these dogs are at a greater risk for inherited diseases such as hip dysplasia and PRA (progressive retinal atrophy), which can lead to blindness.

Some rescued dogs may have behavioral issues. If the problem is a severe one like aggression, and you are a novice dog owner, do not try to adopt him. Let the shelter staff, trainers, and behaviorists work with him and allow a more seasoned dog owner to adopt him. However, if the behavioral issue is something you and the shelter staff are confident can be overcome with some TLC, training, and/or behavioral modification, then by all means bring the Lab into your home. With time and care he should develop into a well-adjusted member of the family.

THE DECISION PROCESS

When thinking about adopting a Lab, make sure you spend time with him outside of his kennel. Dogs will act very differently in a location where they are surrounded by barking dogs than they would in a quiet room.

When you first meet, do not run up to the Lab and try to shower him with affection. He may be a little shy at first. This is acceptable, but if he remains fearful and cowers away from you, or becomes unruly and aggressive, then this is not the right Lab for you. If he is friendly—even if initially hesitant—and comes toward you in that happy Lab way of his, then you are both off to a great start.

The next step is to take him for a walk. You'll want to see how he reacts to you and the leash. If he's a puller, you want to know this ahead of time so you can immediately hire a trainer to work on correcting this behavior.

If he knows any commands, try them and watch how he reacts. Again, if he becomes unruly or he tries to challenge your authority in a manner that makes you uncomfortable, you will need to continue searching for another dog.

CHOOSING A VET

Once you've chosen your Labrador Retriever, whether it is a puppy or a more mature dog, you'll want to make sure that he remains healthy. It is important to choose a veterinarian with whom both you and your dog are comfortable. You will want to choose a vet before bringing your dog—puppy or adult—home, because you should take your Lab to the vet within the first 24 hours for an introduction and an overall health check.

Start your search for a veterinarian by asking where your dog-owning friends, family and neighbors take their dogs and what it is they like about their veterinary clinic. Ask specifically about any emergency situations they may have gone through with their dog at the clinic. Was the staff compassionate and caring? Did they provide updates on a regular basis?

You may also want to get recommendations from your breeder, adoption agency, or local shelter. Look for a clinic that is a member of the American Animal Hospital Association (AAHA). Veterinary clinics that are part of the AAHA are regularly inspected and must meet

Veterinarians that are members of the AAHA are held to a higher standard than those who aren't members. Look for the AAHA logo (above).

specific standards laid out by the organization.

Think about location, but do not base your final decision on this. You may find you are more comfortable with the clinic that is 20 minutes away versus the one around the corner from your home. The veterinarian's office should not be more than a half-hour away. If there is an emergency, you may need to get there quickly.

Once you have narrowed down your potential prospects, give each one a call to find out if they will take on new patients and get more information about the facility. Explain to the receptionist that you are about to bring home a new dog and that you are in need of a veterinarian. Ask about their fees, which can vary greatly from clinic to clinic. Ask what their hours are, the services they provide, the number of veterinarians on staff, and their specialty areas, if they have any.

As the owner of a Labrador Retriever, you may want to consider looking for a veterinarian who is an expert in canine orthopedic issues, as

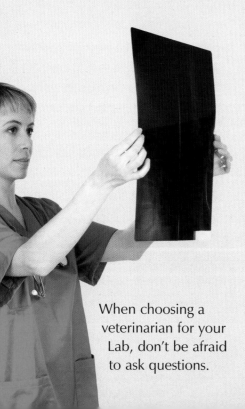

When choosing a veterinarian for your Lab, don't be afraid to ask questions.

Labs are prone to tears of the cruciate ligament in their knees, as well as hip dysplasia. Having a regular vet who specializes in these conditions will come in handy if your Lab develops any of these problems.

The initial phone interview will not only give you some high-level information about the clinic, but it will also give you an idea of their customer service. If the person answering the phone is rushed and rude to you, it may be an indication of how the practice operates. That's probably not the clinic for you. The front-end staff, technicians, and veterinarians should be conscientious, thorough, and kind to you and your dog.

TAKE A TOUR

Once you have narrowed down your choice of potential clinics to one or two, ask to take a tour. A good clinic will have no problem with a potential client visiting their facility.

When you first enter the clinic, pay attention to how you are greeted. Look around the reception area—is it clean and tidy, and are there up-to-date pet magazines? Is there a notice board with posters for lost pets, or posters offering pets to good homes? Are there thank-you cards on the front counter? Those cards provide great references, because they are from people who were extremely satisfied with their pet's care.

You also want to check out the clinic's cleanliness. There should not be any dirt or stray medical supplies lying around. Ask to see all parts of the clinic. Your dog will no doubt have to be x-rayed at some point in his life, so knowing how the room looks and is kept is not an unreasonable request. The same goes for the operating room. If you're bringing home a puppy, he will probably be neutered eventually, so you'll want to see what the OR looks like.

FINAL CHOICE

Once you have made your clinic visits and evaluated all of the information, you need to make your final decision and book an initial appointment with the vet. This should take place within 24 hours of your new Lab coming home.

It will take time to build a relationship with your vet, so don't be afraid to ask questions and get further clarifications on anything you don't fully understand. A good vet will always explain things and make sure you completely understand everything that is going on with your dog, in good health and bad.

If possible, always book non-emergency appointments with the same veterinarian. This will help you build a relationship, and ensure that one doctor becomes very familiar with your dog.

CHAPTER FIVE

What to Expect During the First Six Months

Before your new family member comes home, you have to get your house ready and prepare your family for the lifestyle change that is about to take place.

Once you know the day you will bring home your puppy, plan to take some time off work. The more time you have to spend with your puppy when you first bring him home, the

If your children leave toys lying around where your Labrador Retriever puppy can reach them, they will become his.

easier the transition will be for him, and you. You can also get him off to a great start in terms of housetraining. Being home for the first week is ideal, but not always possible. If you can take a few days off and make a long weekend out of the event, you are still going to be off to a great start.

You may think getting a puppy over the Christmas holidays is a great idea because you will be home. But that's not necessarily true. There may be so much going on during the holidays that you just don't have the opportunity to create a routine for your puppy, and establishing a routine is essential to training him.

PUPPY PROOFING YOUR HOME

Labs are curious and explore the world around them via their mouths. This means that Labs, when given the opportunity, will sniff, carry around, and chew a lot of things they should not. It can cost a lot of money to replace shoes and furniture, as well as to have a small foreign object removed from your puppy. So the first thing you need to do is to get down on your hands and knees and view your home from puppy level, to see what kind of trouble he can cause.

Move any items of value or things that may be dangerous to your puppy out of his reach. Dangling cords from lamps, computers, televisions, and other appliances need to be tied up and hidden, where possible, so your curious canine can't chew through or pull on them. If you can't stash the cords out of your puppy's reach, spray a product such as Bitter Apple onto the cords. These products are all natural, taste terrible to most dogs,

Many common plants can make dogs sick, so watch what your Lab is chewing.

and are meant to deter a dog from chewing the item on which it is sprayed. Bitter Apple and other similar products can be used on virtually everything—including chair and table legs, baseboards, and even your hands—which helps during your puppy's nipping phase.

You need to clear your floors. You can't leave magazines and newspapers lying around the living room and expect them to be readable when you come back 30 seconds later. Puppies love to shred paper, and do it with amazing quickness.

If you have children, it is imperative that their toys not be left lying around, especially if they have small pieces, which can be easily ingested by the puppy and may pose a choking hazard. You also don't want your puppy to make all of your children's toys into his own. Put the children's toys in a room and close the door so the puppy can't get at them. A good rule of thumb to follow is: if it's on the floor, it belongs to the dog.

If your home is filled with flowers and plants, you need to do some research to determine whether they are dangerous to dogs. Labs love to nibble on greenery, so where possible place plants out of reach. Some

Although this chocolate Lab puppy looks adorable, he must be carefully supervised. Keep your pet out of places where he can get into trouble, like the garage, basement, or bathrooms.

potentially toxic houseplants include the asparagus fern, Boston ivy, calla lily, and philodendron.

OFF-LIMITS AREAS

Before your puppy comes home, you need to determine which rooms he will be allowed into and which ones will be strictly off limits. He should not be allowed to roam the whole house until he is fully housetrained, as he needs to be under a constant watchful eye. The rooms he will probably be allowed to go into might include your bedroom, where he will sleep at night in the crate, as well as the kitchen and living room.

In your bedroom, put your dirty laundry in the closet and shut the door. Your shoes also need to go in the closet. Labs love to chew items that smell like their owners, especially dirty laundry and expensive shoes. Also, be sure to clean under your bed, as your Lab will be small enough to wriggle under there and get into trouble.

Kitchens and bathrooms are filled with toxic products, and even though they are kept in the cupboards, these may not be safe. Labs are crafty, and when given the opportunity they can pry open a cupboard door and get into the cleaning products. Keep the cupboard doors securely closed with child locks.

Make sure garbage cans are kept in securely closed cupboards, as Labs love to scour the garbage for scraps.

In the bathroom, keep the toilet lid down so your puppy doesn't develop a habit of drinking from the bowl—or try to use it as a swimming hole. Also, you may initially need to put the toilet paper out of your puppy's reach, as a dangling piece of toilet paper makes for a great toy. Dogs love to grab the paper and run around the house with it, then take a nap on the soft pile of paper they just created.

Harmful products are not only found in kitchens and bathrooms, but also in garages and basements. Products like antifreeze, old paint, fertilizer, insect repellent, motor oil, and turpentine are all toxic to dogs. Saws, hedge clippers, and power tools can also be dangerous to a curious puppy. Restricting your puppy's access to the basement and garage is the safest solution.

BACKYARD

No doubt your new dog will be spending a lot of time playing outside in the backyard. Your Lab should not be left outside for hours on end, but it is okay to let him play and nap unsupervised for short periods of time, as long as the yard is fenced and puppy-proofed.

To puppy-proof your backyard, you first need to remove all poisonous plants as well as dangerous or toxic lawn and garden products. It is important that your fence be secure from top to bottom. Labs can be jumpers, so your fence needs to be at least six feet high, and there should not be any chairs or tables near it that the dog could use as launching pads. The bottom of your fence needs to be flush with the ground. If there are any spaces between the fence and ground, your puppy will do his best to wiggle through and explore the neighbor's backyard.

You need to affix a lock to the gate to deter strangers from coming into the yard and taking your puppy. You also need to repair any holes and loose boards so your dog can't escape from the yard.

If you have a pool or hot tub in your backyard, you must enclose it with a strong wooden or chain-link fence and never let your dog into the backyard without proper supervision. Pool covers are particularly dangerous, as they can fool the dog into thinking the surface is solid. The dog may walk out onto the cover and sink. The cover can collapse onto the dog and suffocate him.

A strong fence should also surround your vegetable garden, so your dog doesn't eat all of your tomatoes or dig up your carrots.

You need to decide if your dog is going to have a designated "bathroom" area in the yard, or if he will be permitted to freely eliminate on your nice green lawn, which will quickly turn yellow in spots and become pockmarked with "landmines."

FINDING THE RIGHT CRATE

Not only do you have to clean up your house and yard in preparation for your new family member, you also have to buy some very important supplies—toys, food, bowls, treats, beds, and a crate.

When used properly, a crate makes a wonderful housetraining tool, as well as a safe place for your puppy to go when you can't supervise him. It's the equivalent of a playpen for children. There are two types of crates suitable for indoor use with puppies and adult dogs—plastic and metal. No matter the size of your Lab, the crate must be roomy enough for him to easily stand up, turn around, and stretch out.

The hard plastic crates come in various sizes, so expect to buy one or two to get you through the housetraining phase, as Labs come home weighing anywhere from five to 12 pounds (two to five kg) on average

Introduce your puppy to his crate in a positive way. As he grows he may come to know it as his "home," so it's important to keep any references to the crate positive. Never confine your Lab to the crate as punishment for bad behavior.

and grow to about 80 pounds (36 kg) within the first year, which is how long housetraining can last. Buying just one plastic crate intended to house your Lab both as a puppy and an adult is not wise. It will be too big initially, and this will hamper the potty training that the crate is supposed to help facilitate. Dogs have a natural instinct to not do their business where they sleep and eat, so a properly sized crate teaches a puppy to hold his bladder muscle for as long as he possibly can, and become accustomed to regular bathroom breaks.

Plastic crates don't allow your puppy to easily see what is going on around him, which may make him feel isolated from the family. Wire crates, on the other hand, allow your dog to see all around him, so he feels like he is a part of the action without being in the middle of it. They also come with a divider, which means you can buy one large crate, but use the divider to give your puppy just the right amount of room.

INTRODUCING THE CRATE

Your puppy may or may not have been in a crate before you brought him home. If he has never been in one, make the introduction slowly and positively. If the toys inside the crate don't entice him to check things out, lure him into it with a treat or his meal, then quietly close the door. You don't want to slam it shut and startle the puppy. Leave him in there for a few minutes then let him out. Gradually increase the amount of time you keep him in the crate so he gets the idea that this is his place.

A puppy should never be left in the crate for more than two to four hours at a time, except overnight. Puppies can generally last a bit longer at night without needing a bathroom break.

When leaving treats in the crate to occupy your puppy for a couple of hours, use a non-edible, extra-durable chew product or dispenser. You never want to leave your dog unattended with a rawhide-type product as he could choke on it. The same goes for stuffed toys. Labs love to destroy soft toys, but they can easily choke on the stuffing.

Do not leave water in the crate as it can be consumed very quickly, resulting in your puppy needing to relieve himself much sooner than planned. Alternately, the bowl will get dumped and soak the bed, making it uncomfortable for your Labrador Retriever to lie on over the next few hours.

A word of caution about crates: never put a dog of any size or age into the crate with his collar on. A noise outside the house can frighten him and depending on the severity of the fright, your Lab may become stressed to the point of trying to escape the crate. While he is trying to escape the crate, his collar can get caught on some part of the crate and choke him.

You never want to put your dog in the crate as punishment. The crate, when used properly, is your puppy's safe haven, not his time-out room.

PICKING UP YOUR PUPPY

Finally, the day arrives when the breeder will permit you to pick up your new puppy. By doing your research, puppy proofing your home, and having the necessary supplies on hand for his arrival, you have done all you can to prepare yourself for the playful bundle of fur.

Remember to bring a leash and collar with you to the breeder's, along with a crate for him to ride in on the way home. If you can, get an old towel or some other piece of fabric from the breeder that has the scent of the dog's mom and littermates on it and place it in the crate. It will help make the separation a little less stressful.

When you first bring your puppy home, keep him on a leash. It will take months before you can allow him to freely roam around the house. First, he needs to be taught the rules, which include what he is permitted to chew and, most importantly, that he does his business outside, not in the house.

When you pick up your puppy from a reputable breeder, she will provide you with a lot of information on him, including paperwork verifying that he has been cleared of specific diseases. Two certificates you must receive from your breeder—and again, a reputable breeder will supply them without question in the puppy package—are the CERF (Canine Eye Registration Foundation) and OFA (Orthopedic Foundation for Animals), or Wind-Morgan or PennHIP, certifications for the puppy and his parents.

YOUR DOG'S PAPERS

Having an American Kennel Club–registered puppy does not mean you have a superior Lab when compared to someone else's, or that he is more valuable than another dog. AKC registration also does not mean that he is healthier or bred better than another Lab, and it does not mean your Lab is show quality. All an AKC registration means is that your puppy is a purebred.

When you buy from a breeder, your AKC registration will either be limited or full. A limited registration means that you are not allowed to breed the puppy and have the litter registered with the AKC. In essence, you and the breeder are agreeing that this puppy will become a family pet only. Limited registered Labs cannot be show dogs.

Full registration, on the other hand, means that the breeder gives the owner permission to show the dog. This also means the dog does not have to be spayed or neutered.

You, not the breeder, are responsible for registering the puppy with the American Kennel Club. However, a breeder may help with the registration after certain requirements of your contract are fulfilled (for example, if you send her proof that your puppy has been spayed or neutered). The breeder will then complete the AKC registration form and send you the puppy's papers.

What's the difference between a dog's pedigree and AKC registration? The pedigree outlines the puppy's family tree, whereas the AKC papers prove your puppy is a purebred.

Many breeders have their Labs certified against elbow and hip dysplasia, as this breed is prone to both conditions. The OFA hip and elbow certifications are good for the life of your dog. If your dog gets hip or elbow dysplasia at some point in his life, you should contact the breeder and tell her so she can further investigate the dog's lineage. The CERF declares that the puppy's eyes are free of disease. It must be updated on an annual basis.

Other paperwork your breeder will provide you with includes his vaccination records and his parents' health certificates, pedigree, and AKC papers.

SALES CONTRACT

A reputable breeder will require you to sign a contract, which will also serve as your bill of sale.

Stipulations in the contract will include the "right of first refusal" clause, which gives the breeder the option to take the dog back if you are no longer able to care for him. A breeder will sometimes interpret the clause as optional on her part, so she may actually refuse to take the dog back. However, a truly reputable breeder should take him back six months or six years down the road for any reason. If you return the dog to the breeder, don't expect a refund.

The contract will stipulate that the breeder guarantees that her puppy is healthy, does not suffer from any illnesses or parasites, and is free from hereditary defects.

Your obligations under the contract will probably include taking your puppy to a veterinarian within a specified amount of time (usually 24 to 48 hours). If by any chance health issues are discovered at this visit, the breeder may offer you a refund or a replacement puppy. However, this will depend upon the ailment and will be at the breeder's discretion.

The contract will also stipulate that you care for your dog in an appropriate manner and that you will spay or neuter your puppy by a certain age—usually no later than 12 months of age.

If you are interested in stud or breeding rights for your puppy, this must be discussed with your breeder prior to choosing your puppy and signing the contract.

WHAT TO EXPECT THE FIRST FEW NIGHTS AND MONTHS

The first few days and nights following your puppy's arrival will be overwhelming, tiring, confusing, frustrating, but above all, wonderful. Your puppy will know nothing—including his name, how to sit on cue, come, or relieve himself in the proper location. These are things you will have to slowly and patiently teach him. As time goes by, you will notice that he responds to his name when you call him, sits when you ask him to, and eliminates in his designated outside location. But be patient—these things won't happen overnight and he may not have accomplished some of these things by six months of age.

The first night may be the worst night for everyone, as this will be the first time your puppy is forced to get through the night in a strange place without his mother or littermates. Expect him to cry and whine.

There are a few things you can do to make the first night a little less stressful. Put your puppy's crate beside your bed, as knowing that someone even a little bit familiar is close by will comfort him. Put the piece of clothing you got from the breeder in the crate with him, as the scent of his mother and littermates will give him additional comfort. Because he has no littermates to snuggle with for comfort and warmth, place a warm water bottle wrapped in a towel in the crate with him. This will replicate their body warmth. There are also dog toys with a warmer and heartbeat inside available that may help your puppy feel less lonely.

YOUR PUPPY'S HEALTH

Within the first 24 to 48 hours of bringing your puppy home, you need to take him to the vet for an exam.

Don't be surprised if your puppy is forlorn during his first night at home. You can help reduce his fear and loneliness by moving his crate into your room.

This first visit introduces your new puppy to your veterinary clinic in a friendly and nonthreatening manner; it should give your puppy a positive first impression of the vet, the clinic, and its staff.

When you go for this visit, bring your puppy's vaccination records, as well as a stool sample. The stool sample will enable the vet to check your puppy for parasites. You will also be asked to fill out forms detailing your contact information

FAST FACT

Everyone in your family and neighborhood is going to want to meet the newest member of your family. Your puppy will love all of the attention, but make sure visitors leave their own dogs at home at first. An eight-week-old puppy has a very weak immune system, and is not ready to be around unfamiliar dogs.

and your Lab's information (such as gender, color, and age). Arrive at the appointment a few minutes early so you have enough time to complete the paperwork.

The veterinarian will perform a high-level exam to ensure your puppy is healthy. He will check your Lab's heart and lungs, eyes, ears, and range of motion in his limbs. For Labs, the range of motion test is very important, as it can reveal looseness in the hips, which could be a precursor to hip dysplasia.

Your vet will go through your puppy's vaccination schedule with you. Over the next four months, your puppy will receive numerous inoculations to help him fend off potential diseases. Vaccinating your puppy is imperative, as the vaccines are designed to trigger your puppy's naturally occurring protective

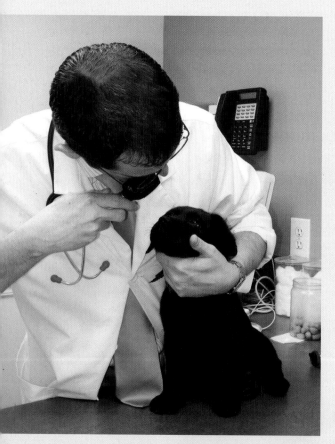

An eye exam will be part of your veterinarian's initial puppy health screening.

immune responses in an effort to protect himself from disease.

The most important vaccines include parvovirus, distemper, and rabies.

CANINE PARVOVIRUS: This disease, also known as parvo, is highly infectious and its effects can include severe vomiting, bloody diarrhea, a high fever, dehydration, and depression. It has a 50 percent mortality rate.

Parvo is transmitted through fecal matter and can live in the soil for up to a year. It can also survive on the bottom of your shoes and on dogs' paws for upwards of 10 days.

Puppies receive a minimum of three doses of the vaccine between six and 16 weeks of age at three to four-week intervals. Your puppy should have received his first parvo vaccine while still in the breeder's care.

CANINE DISTEMPER: Distemper is another potentially fatal disease. It is highly contagious and is transmitted through the air, as well as by shoes and clothes.

Symptoms of distemper are a yellowish-grey discharge from your puppy's nose and eyes, which is accompanied by a dry cough, lethargy, and a fever. Other symptoms include

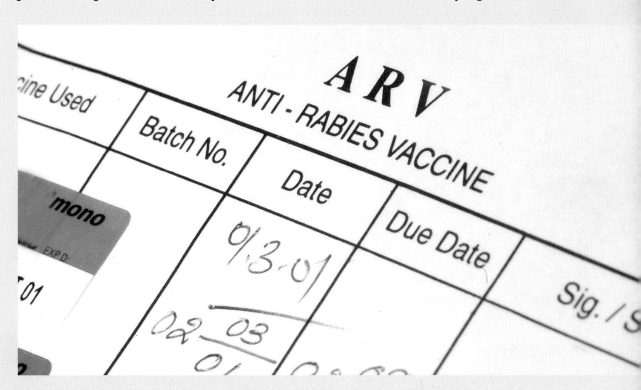

Every municipality requires dogs to be vaccinated against rabies.

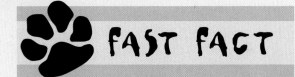

vomiting, diarrhea, and a loss of appetite. As the disease progresses, it can attack the Lab's intestinal tract and nervous system, resulting in seizures and convulsions.

The vaccination protocol requires puppies to receive a minimum of three doses between six and 16 weeks of age. Your breeder's veterinarian should have given your puppy his initial vaccination at six weeks of age. The remaining vaccines occur every three to four weeks.

RABIES: All municipalities in North America require dogs to be vaccinated against rabies, because this disease is almost always fatal to the dog and can have serious ramifications for people. A person can contract rabies by coming into contact with the dog's saliva either through a bite or by the saliva entering an open wound.

There are actually two forms of the rabies disease, both of which attack a dog's central nervous system. The dumb, or paralytic, form of rabies causes paralysis of the dog's throat, resulting in excessive drooling, as well as the inability to swallow. The other form, furious rabies, makes the infected dog go "mad," becoming vicious and attacking anything. Furious rabies will eventually cause paralysis in the dog, which is followed by death within a few days.

Rabies vaccines are available in a one-year and a three-year vaccine. Either vaccination can be given to a puppy as young as three months of age.

OTHER VACCINATIONS

If you plan to put your puppy into doggie daycare, you may be required to give him a bordetella vaccine, which will help him stave off kennel cough.

Kennel cough is highly infectious and is transmitted through the air. It will not harm a healthy dog, but it can be dangerous to a puppy. It is characterized by a dry, hacking cough. The bordetella vaccine is administered in two doses—one when the puppy is between six and eight weeks of age and another one when he is between 10 and 12 weeks old.

PUPPY NUTRITION

Puppies are born with an undeveloped immune system, but by nursing

Puppies start out eating nothing but mother's milk.

from their mother, puppies are able to obtain colostrum, which contain antibodies, electrolytes, proteins, and vitamins, all of which are important in protecting him from infection and disease.

When puppies are born, they feed every two hours and should gain weight every day for the first three weeks. At about three weeks of age, the breeder will start feeding the puppies three to four times a day a mush that is comprised of ground puppy kibble, liquid milk replacement, and water. Over the next four weeks, the breeder will decrease the mush's milk replacement and water content, so that by the time the puppies are seven

weeks old they are eating only dry puppy kibble.

It is important to keep your new puppy on the same diet for the first few days to avoid an upset stomach. When you pick up your puppy from the breeder, she may supply you with a bit of the food she has been feeding the puppies. If the breeder

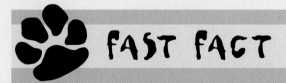

Feeding your Lab a poor-quality diet can lead to nutritional deficiencies. Dry skin, a dull or poor coat, and behavioral issues may all be signs that your dog is not getting the proper nutrition.

does not give you any of the kibble, find out what kind it is and make sure to have some on hand before his next meal. You may also want to get a container of the breeder's water to mix in with yours, for the same reason.

Over time, you may decide to change your puppy's food. With so many different kinds—kibble, semi-soft, frozen, and canned—available, the choices may seem overwhelming. Don't worry, though—you don't need a degree in canine nutrition. There is no one brand that is best for one particular breed, so you will have to do some research. Talk to your local pet food store staff and ask what they recommend for Labs. Their recommendations will be based on product quality and customer feedback.

When you read the dog food label, look for a few things. It should have an AAFCO (American

Association of Feed Control Officials) stamp of approval. This means the food is nutritionally balanced and complete according to the AAFCO guidelines. AAFCO foods must contain certain vitamins and minerals in proper proportion, and have successfully passed feed trial tests. If the label does not state it meets the AAFCO guidelines, then keep looking.

You also want to choose a food that is specifically formulated for large breed puppies. A large breed puppy is defined as a breed of dog that will grow to weigh more than 50 pounds as an adult. These foods are formulated to help Labs grow at a slow and steady rate, which will help lessen their chances of suffering from musculoskeletal disorders (in particular, hip and elbow dysplasia). Growing too quickly will only increase the likelihood of your puppy one day suffering from one of these debilitating conditions.

Large breed puppy foods contain less calcium when compared to other dog foods, which helps to regulate their bone growth. These foods will most likely have glucosamine and

Dry kibble may be the healthiest choice for your pet. In addition to giving your Labrador Retriever the nutrition he requires, it will also help to keep his teeth clean.

chondroitan added to them, both of which are believed to help improve a large breed dog's joint cartilage.

DIETARY OPTIONS

Labs love to eat, and they eat a lot. Most Labs are fed a dry kibble-based diet, as this is convenient and economical. Kibble has the added benefit of helping to cut down on plaque and tartar build-up on your Lab's teeth.

Choose a kibble formula for large breed puppies, and make sure that it's made from high-quality ingredients. Avoid vegetable-based kibbles—dogs are carnivores and do better with a meat-based diet. (At least two of the first five ingredients listed must be meat in order for the food to qualify as meat-based.) Vegetable-based diets, which are made mostly of rice, wheat, and corn, are less expensive per bag than the meat-based ones. However, they will be more expensive in the long run, as you will have to feed your Lab more of the lesser-quality food per meal in order to meet his nutritional requirements. Vegetable diets are also very high in carbohydrates, which are difficult for dogs to digest.

You want to check how the food is preserved. Today, most dog foods are naturally preserved with vitamin E and, in some cases, vitamin C.

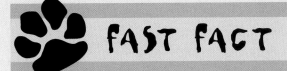

FAST FACT

In recent years, many people have opted to put their puppies on raw food diets. There is a lot of controversy surrounding this diet, so you must do research and consult your veterinarian before you feed your puppy raw foods.

Avoid foods that use chemical preservatives, such as ethoxyquin, as they can actually be harmful to dogs.

If you want to feed your Labrador Retriever natural foods, you may want to consider feeding him a frozen diet. These foods are made with fresh meat, vegetables, and fruit, and contain nothing artificial. The food is easy to feed, as it can be cut into chunks once it is thawed. On the other hand, frozen dog food is expensive and not always easy to find.

Avoid giving your puppy semi-soft dog food as his main nutritional source. This type of food is a serious downgrade from kibble or frozen dog food because it is made with sugar, animal tissues, grains, and fats—it's essentially junk food for dogs.

On the other hand, canned foods can be nutritionally complete because they are made with one or two types of muscle meats or poultry, as well as animal by-products, grains, vitamins, and minerals. Canned food is best when combined with a puppy's kibble, especially if he is having difficulties chewing. However, canned foods are high in calories and fat, and are expensive.

Semi-soft and canned foods also don't help reduce plaque and tartar build-up on your dog's teeth. If you feed your Lab a soft diet, you may find yourself having to pay for professional teeth cleaning on a regular basis.

FEEDING

Puppies must be fed at regular intervals. Initially, he will need to be fed three times a day—breakfast, lunch, and dinner. Between five and six months of age, you can start feeding your puppy twice a day—breakfast and dinner. Make the transition gradually over a one-week period by slowly decreasing the amount of food you give him at lunchtime and increasing his food allotment in the morning and evening.

Labs eat quite vigorously, but this zest for meals can put their health at risk. In particular, they can suffer from bloat, which occurs when the dog's stomach enlarges because of too much gas. Another cause of bloat is the stomach inexplicably twisting (torsion). Bloat is almost always fatal unless emergency medical attention is immediately sought.

Because Labs have deep chests, they are susceptible to bloat. But there are steps you can take to minimize the risk. Keep your dog quiet (not active) for at least a half-hour before each meal. Don't allow your Lab to drink a lot of water after eating dry kibble, and try not to feed a kibble that expands greatly once it becomes wet. (You can test this by soaking the kibble in water overnight; this will indicate how much the kibble will swell in your dog's stomach.) All of these precautions are designed to slow down your Lab's eating. You also want your dog to rest for 30 minutes following a meal. Once he has done his business, bring him back in the house and have him lay on his bed. This is a routine you should start from the first meal. He will quickly catch on and oblige.

Never put a bowl of food down in the morning and allow your puppy to pick at it throughout the day. This is called free feeding, or grazing. For one thing, the typical Lab will eat everything in a matter of minutes. Also, you need to always remind your Lab that you are his boss, and a surefire way to do this is by being his food source. This will be of particular importance when your Lab is going through his "terrible twos" and adolescent phases—two times when he will challenge your authority.

Although grazing is not allowed, you should always have fresh water available for your Lab.

YOUR DEVELOPING DOG

Your puppy is going to go through a lot of physical, social, and intellectual changes over the next few months. Think of it as experiencing a child's infancy, "terrible twos," adolescence, and puberty all within a six-month time frame instead of 16 years.

When your puppy comes home, he will be in the midst of his infancy stage (eight to 12 weeks of age). During this stage of his life, he is solely concerned with satisfying his basic needs—eating, sleeping, eliminating, and playing. Don't expect much during these first few weeks. If he will come to you when you call his name two days in a row, then consider yourself lucky. But, for the most part, he won't be able to remember anything from one day to the next.

Between eight and 10 weeks of age, your puppy will go through a very important stage—the fear-impression period—of his emotional development. All of a sudden he might become

When introducing your puppy to a child, show the child how to be gentle and avoid causing fear.

afraid of anything and everything. If this is left unchecked, he may grow up to become a very fearful dog.

To help minimize his fear, teach your children never to chase and poke your puppy, especially with noisy items like the vacuum hose. Most importantly, when the puppy exhibits a fear of something, do not coddle, pet, or comfort him. He will think you are also frightened of the object or situation, and that being afraid is okay. You want to ignore his fear and let your puppy investigate the situation on his own terms. It may take a few tries, but with patience he will overcome these fears.

THREE TO FOUR MONTHS OF AGE

Around 10 weeks of age, your easy-going, happy-go-lucky, follow-you-around-everywhere puppy becomes more comfortable with his surroundings, and will become more brave and bold. During this phase—which is the equivalent of a child's "terrible two" stage—he will become very demanding. Your Lab will want to be the center of your attention at all times and will do whatever is necessary to get you to notice him. This can include pawing at you while you're watching TV, or going into the laundry hamper and bringing you a pair

of soiled underwear when you're entertaining dinner guests.

You have to remember that, to a puppy, any attention is good, whether you are praising him or scolding him. You are better off ignoring the bad and praising the good.

During this phase, he will also test your position as the household's top dog. Your puppy instinctively wants to overthrow you and become the pack leader. He will challenge you every chance he gets, but you must not let him win.

This is where puppy school comes into play. At around three months old, believe it or not, your Lab's brain is fully developed and he's starting to learn things, both good and bad. You will have taught him some things, but he will learn many things on his own.

It is important to start training him to do what you want him to do, and this includes redirecting his bad behaviors towards appropriate ones. He will act like a tough guy, but he's still young and impressionable enough to be taught right from wrong.

With diligent training and strict enforcement of your household rules, you will be on your way to having a great Lab. Everyone will fawn over him and gush about how well behaved he is—until the day he decides being obedient is no longer on his to-do list.

ADOLESCENCE

This personality flip usually occurs around five months of age. This is the equivalent of a child's adolescent phase. Just as teenagers can be bratty, defiant, and strong-willed, so too can a five or six-month old Labrador Retriever.

How do you know you've hit the teenage stage? Instead of walking amicably beside you as you go around the block, your Lab will try to pull you around the neighbor-

hood. He won't come when he's called, and instead will look at you, then take off in the opposite direction. When you correct him, his bad behavior will actually become worse, not better.

It is important that you continue to attend obedience classes during this phase, or at the very least maintain a regular training schedule at home, as the lessons will help to remind your Lab who the boss really is—you, not him.

Take a look at it from your Lab's point of view. He's growing (he should be about two-thirds of his

When your Lab puppy is about five months old, he will probably start testing his boundaries. Stick to your training schedule, or enroll in obedience classes, and you'll get through this stage in his development.

adult size); the world isn't as scary as it once was; and he is naturally curious. Therefore, he wants to get out there and explore it all. You may not think you can get through this phase, but you will. Be patient. He will eventually come around.

SOCIALIZATION

In order for your puppy to become a well-adjusted adult dog, you must expose him to every kind of person, other cats and dogs, household noise and social situation you can imagine. If you don't properly socialize your puppy, you risk having a fearful or aggressive adult Lab on your hands, which isn't much fun for you when out for a walk or entertaining guests.

When socializing him, you have to keep in mind that puppies have immature immune systems and, therefore, are very susceptible to disease, especially before they've received all of their vaccinations. This does not mean you must keep your puppy locked up in the house for the first few months of his life. It just means that when you take him outside of the house, or have people over, you must take certain precautions.

Numerous parasites and diseases are carried around on the bottom of our shoes, so when you come home and when people come into your home, make sure everyone takes their shoes off at the door. You and your guests should always wash your hands before handling the puppy. You also want to hide the shoes as your Lab will want to chew them—they love everybody's shoes.

When out walking your puppy, you will no doubt come across other dog owners doing the very same thing. However, you would be best to avoid the canine greeting ritual until your puppy has received all of his vaccines or your veterinarian says it's okay.

Even if you don't have children, it's important for your puppy to be exposed to kids. These first experiences must be positive, so you need to be in control of the introduction. Before you let a child pet your puppy, show the child how to do it gently. You also want children, and adults, to come down to the puppy's level so they are not intimidating to him. Avoid allowing your puppy to be swarmed by a gaggle of children. All of these new, noisy, and excitable people can be overwhelming.

If at any point your puppy becomes fearful when you are introducing him to new people, don't push the situation. This will only cause your puppy to become more agitated and frightened. Instead, remove your Lab from the situation.

You don't want your Lab to run and hide behind the couch every time you turn the blender on. A good and reputable breeder will raise her puppies in the house, so they should be accustomed to regular household noises, such as the vacuum or the banging of pots and pans.

GROOMING

Although Labrador Retrievers are relatively low-maintenance when it comes to grooming, there are certain things you need to do on a regular basis for aesthetic reasons, but also for the health of your dog. The best time to learn about your Lab's body is when he's a puppy. Touching your puppy all over will help veterinary exams go smoothly, as he will become accustomed to being touched by people. It will also help facilitate the bonding process.

It will be hard for you to keep your hands off your cute, cuddly, and soft puppy, so while petting him you can also do a "lump and bump" check. You're essentially looking for anything abnormal. If you start doing this from day one, you will get a sense of what is normal and not normal for your dog.

Labs may have short fur, but they have an abundance of it. They are renowned for their double-coat—a soft undercoat, which is coupled with a coarse, wiry outer layer. While they shed all year long, they molt—a significant shedding of hair—twice a year, once when the weather warms up in the spring, and again when the weather turns colder in the fall.

Not only will brushing your Lab on a regular basis (once a week) help the shedding process, regular brushing will also help remove any dirt embedded in the fur as well as spread out the fur's natural oils, leaving his coat soft and shiny.

Labs love water, but that does not mean they should be frequently bathed. In fact, your Lab should be

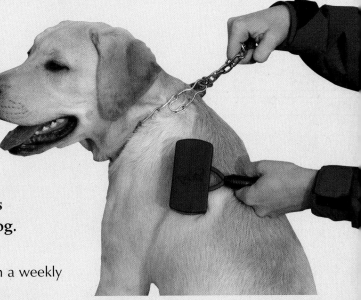

Labrador Retrievers should be brushed on a weekly basis to keep their coats tidy and shiny.

bathed infrequently—usually only when he comes home from a run in the forest smelling rather unpleasant. Bathing a dog too often can actually do more harm than good, as it can dry out his skin and coat. When bathing your Lab, use dog shampoo, not a shampoo formulated for people. Even baby shampoo will be too harsh for your dog's coat.

Your dog's gait and how often he walks on hard surfaces, such as concrete, will determine how often you need to trim his nails. Hard surfaces naturally keep dogs' nails short. You will know it's time for a nail trim when you hear your Lab's nails clicking on your kitchen tile or on the sidewalk. Letting his nails grow too long can lead to orthopedic problems, because long nails prevent your dog from walking properly.

Use dog-specific nail trimmers. Nail trimming can be difficult, especially if your Lab has dark nails, which prevent you from seeing the quick. The quick houses the foot's nerve and blood supply, so if you cut the nail too short, you will cause some bleeding. To stop the bleeding,

Hard surfaces help to keep your Lab's nails short, but his nails will still need to be trimmed on a regular basis.

cover the cut nail with styptic powder or flour.

Labs have adorable floppy ears, but these can house some nasty infections. A healthy Lab's ear is pink and odor-free. An infected ear is smelly and filled with a black or dark brown wax. If you notice the odor and/or waxy build-up, make an appointment with your veterinarian. Do not try to treat this at home, as the infection could be either bacterial or viral and these require different treatments.

If there is discolored discharge coming from your puppy's eyes, it may be an environmental irritation, overactive or blocked tear duct, or conjunctivitis. There may even be something in his eye causing the irritation. No matter the cause, do not try to clean it yourself. Instead, contact your veterinarian immediately for an appointment.

TAKING CARE OF THE TEETH

Good canine dental hygiene is just as imperative as our own dental hygiene. A build-up of plaque and tartar can lead to painful tooth decay and expensive extractions. It can also contribute to heart disease in dogs.

Keeping your Lab's chompers pearly white can be as simple as feeding him a kibble-based diet. When a dog chews the hard kibble, the pieces scrape against his teeth,

preventing plaque and tartar from building up on the enamel.

If you have ever watched your Lab eat, you'll know that he is more likely to gulp down his food without a thorough chewing. So that your dog can get the cleaning benefits of the kibble, many dog food manufacturers have created larger-sized kibble that a Lab will have to chew before swallowing. Some companies even tag these foods as having oral health benefits right on the bag. If you decide to feed your dog this type of food, make sure it is nutritionally appropriate. If you do not want to change his diet, buy a small bag and use the larger kibble as treats.

There are numerous treats available to help with canine oral hygiene. Rawhides and bones are the tried and true favorites of Labs, as they are not easily chewed apart.

Perhaps the most effective way to prevent plaque and tartar from accumulating is to brush your dog's teeth. Brushing should be done at least three times a week. There are numerous dog toothpastes available in all kinds of yummy flavors, such as chicken, beef, and peanut butter. Brushing your dog's teeth may seem over-the-top, but it is effective. When brushing your Lab's teeth, use a regular toothbrush or a finger brush. Both work equally well.

Don't be afraid to put your finger in his mouth. This is something you should have been doing since day one anyway in order to make him comfortable with you taking things away from him. Also, don't try to save a few dollars by using your own toothpaste on your pet. Human toothpastes are laced with numerous chemicals that are inappropriate for dogs, not to mention a minty flavor that most dogs don't like.

Like humans, some dogs are just prone to having problematic teeth and no matter what you do, plaque and tartar will build up. In these cases, a professional cleaning by your veterinarian once a year may be necessary in order to avoid costly and painful extractions down the road.

POTTY TRAINING

Housebreaking a puppy is challenging. It won't happen overnight and it will take a lot of patience and understanding on your part, especially when he has an accident.

Puppies have elimination routines—they go when they first wake up, after they eat, following playtime, and after being confined for a long period of time. Understanding his routine, and learning the signals that he has to go (sniffing a certain spot, standing at the door, or whining in

FAST FACT

When housebreaking your puppy, you will need a lot of paper towels and a good enzymatic cleaner, as there will be a lot of accidents to clean up. Avoid using a cleaner that contains ammonia, as it is a component of urine and its scent will continually attract your puppy to that spot.

his crate), will put you well on your way to housetraining your puppy.

It is important to use military precision in your scheduling of meals and bathroom breaks, as this will help avoid accidents and teach your puppy to hold his urine as long as he physically can. For the most part, puppies ages six to 14 weeks can hold their bladders for only an hour or two, so you will be going outside with him eight to 10 days times a day.

Around the 14-week mark, puppies start to gain a little bit more control over their urges, and you will notice a significant decrease in the number of required bathroom breaks your puppy will need each day.

At this age, he may have more control over his bladder muscles, but you cannot expect your puppy to hold it all day. He will continue to require one or two mid-day bathroom and exercise breaks daily. If you are unable to come home throughout the day, hire a professional pet sitter or ask a friend or neighbor to come by for scheduled breaks.

When teaching your puppy to eliminate outside, take him to the same location each time and use the same phrases to encourage him (such as "go potty," "go pee," "go poop" or "do your business"). When he's done, give him lots of praise and tasty rewards.

As your puppy becomes better at giving you signals and not having accidents, you can increase the amount of free space you give him when you're not home. Do this slowly. If accidents occur, cut back on his free space, as it was likely too much too soon.

Accidents are going to happen—this is a fact of puppy raising. If you walk into a room and find a pile or puddle, clean it up with an enzymatic cleaner and move on. Do not punish your puppy by rubbing his nose in it or scolding him—he won't understand what he did wrong. If you catch your puppy in the act of having an accident, make a noise to get his attention, then quickly scoop him up and bring him to his designated outdoor bathroom. When he's done, praise him, and then clean up the accident.

On average, it will take your puppy about six months to be completely housetrained, then an additional few months of no mistakes in order for you to trust him alone in your house when you're not there. Some dogs will move through this process more quickly or slowly than others. It all depends on your dog and how diligently you have stuck to your housetraining routine.

You have to keep in mind that your Lab puppy is not physically capable of controlling his bladder muscle for long periods of time, and

Be patient with your Lab puppy when he has an accident. Part of being a dog owner involves cleaning the occasional mess, especially during housetraining.

this is not something you can speed along. No matter how long the process takes, you must remain patient and not give up. Most importantly, do not get angry or frustrated at your puppy when he makes mistakes—it's all part of his learning process and he's doing the best he can.

LABS NEED MANNERS TOO

Just as we teach children to have manners and say "please" and "thank you," so too must we teach our Labs the value of having good manners.

Good canine manners consist of not jumping all over you and/or your company when they come through the door; letting you go first, instead of knocking you out of the way, when you both try to go through the door; taking treats from your hand nicely; and obeying any command you give him readily and quickly.

Every time your Lab wants something from you—food, a game of fetch, or a scratch behind the ears—he must first work for it by obeying a command. For example, when giving your Lab a meal, make him sit, then put the bowl down and make him leave it. Then release him with the word "okay" so he can enjoy his food. This is a regular reminder that you are in charge.

Requesting that your dog do something in exchange for something he wants is not bribery, but a great way to make training a regular part of your day, which also provides much-needed mental stimulation for your Lab. This will also go a long way towards helping him understand his place within the family.

If you don't require your Lab to have manners, you are setting yourself up for a struggle of supremacy. Labs have strong personalities and when given the opportunity, they will lay claim to the top dog position in the house.

CHAPTER SIX

Your Lab Is Growing Up

Labrador Retrievers can grow too quickly for their own good, which is why it is important to feed them a proper diet—one specifically formulated for large breed puppies—until they are 12 months old. Once a Lab turns a year old, he can be fed a large breed maintenance formula.

During your puppy's first six months of life, he has gone through a lot of social, emotional, and most notably, physical changes. You are no longer able to scoop your six-month-old Lab into your arms and cradle him like a baby. Instead, every time he bumps into you or steps on your foot, it feels like an elephant encounter.

Right when you think your Lab's growth rate is going to result in you living with a horse, he'll slow down.

Between six months and two years of age, your Labrador Retriever will continue growing and learning.

This occurs around seven months of age, but he is not done growing. At around 10 to 14 months of age, a Labrador Retriever's growth plates will close. However, he will still be filling out for another eight to 12 months, during which time he will gain more muscle mass.

This long growth period leaves your Lab susceptible to numerous bone and joint problems, which is why proper diet is so important.

Throughout a Lab's life, but particularly before he is two years old, he is still growing. Therefore, his diet and weight have to be carefully monitored. Labs love to eat and have a genetic predisposition for obesity. That is why, no matter how long and hard he may beg for more food or snacks, you, as a responsible Lab owner, can't give in.

KEEPING YOUR LAB HEALTHY

Your Lab requires annual check-ups so your veterinarian can ensure he is in good health. The annual visit can also help stave off any serious medical conditions by catching them early.

During the annual exam, your vet will check your Lab's heart and lung function, as well as his weight, pulse and temperature. Ears, eyes, and teeth are all examined for signs of infection. The vet will test your Lab's range of motion to ensure that his limbs are not too stiff or too loose, either of which can lead to orthopedic problems down the road. The vet will also do an overall bump and lump check, as the presence of either may indicate an infection or a tumor.

Your dog will also receive whatever annual vaccines you and your vet

CRATING AN ADULT DOG

Some adult dogs come from homes where they were crated. However, there is the possibility the previous owner misused the crate, thereby leaving a negative impression of it on the dog. Depending on the severity of the dog's reaction to the crate, you may have to forgo it and contain your Lab in a room instead.

If your adult Lab is a jumper, and can easily hurdle over baby gates, then he will have to be housed in the laundry room or another room with tiled flooring and a door until you are able to trust him in the house alone for hours at a time. But if your adult Lab is accepting of the crate, train him the same way you would a puppy.

To keep your Lab in good health, make sure the veterinarian examines him every year.

decided upon when you first brought your puppy into the clinic.

Bring a fecal sample so it can be tested for parasites. While you're at the clinic, blood will be drawn for a heartworm test. A dog clean of parasites can be placed on a heartworm protocol. Heartworms are long, thin worms that get passed to dogs via mosquito bites. The heartworm then develops inside the dog's heart. If not caught in time, heartworms can block blood vessels, leading to breathing complications and eventual heart failure in the dog.

It is imperative that your Lab be put on a heartworm medication, which, depending on the product, may also help to fend off other parasites such as fleas, ear mites, hookworms, and ticks.

Labs are active, big and not always the most coordinated and graceful dogs around, which means you may be visiting your vet's office more than you would like. Don't worry—as you get used to owning a Lab, you will be able to tell which ailments are treatable at home, and which require immediate medical attention from your vet. In either

CANINE FIRST AID

Your canine first aid kit should contain the following items:

- gauze pads
- antibiotic ointment
- hydrogen peroxide
- petroleum jelly
- eye wash
- ear wash
- medications
- bismuth tablets
- sterile stretch gauze
- bandage scissors
- splints

- a blanket
- tweezers
- tensor bandage
- rectal thermometer
- paperwork, including the dog's health record
- medications
- local and national poison control numbers
- phone numbers for your regular veterinary clinic and the emergency clinic.

case, when you notice your Lab is not acting like himself, call the vet so a visit can be scheduled.

EMERGENCIES

Any time your Lab refuses to eat and doesn't want to play, you may have a serious situation on your hands that must be dealt with immediately by your vet.

The cause for your Lab's lessened zest for life could be as simple as an upset stomach, which may be the result of eating something off the counter he shouldn't have, or he may have a foreign object lodged in his intestinal tract.

A good grab off the counter may result in a bout of diarrhea or vomiting, both of which you can treat at home by not giving him any food for 12 to 24 hours. But do provide him with ample amounts of water, as your Lab can become dehydrated.

If the vomiting and diarrhea has blood in it, is projectile, or continues for 24 hours, then you need to contact your vet immediately. But if withholding food for 24 hours seems to be working, slowly reintroduce some very bland foods such as boiled chicken or hamburger, rice, cottage cheese, cooked pasta, or soft-boiled eggs. If the vomiting or diarrhea returns with these foods, go to the vet.

Other emergency situations will likely occur while you and your Lab are having fun outdoors. These dogs are notorious for suffering anterior cruciate ligament (ACL) tears. ACL injuries happen when your Lab suddenly twists or hyper-extends his knee. You will know when this happens as he will either cry out in pain or refuse to place any weight on the injured leg. Surgery is required to fix an ACL tear, with TPLO (tibial plateau lev-eling osteotomy) being the most successful, albeit expensive, option currently available.

Your Lab is also very likely to suf-fer some kind of toe injury, such as a broken, sprained, or dislocated toe. These injuries are usually the result of your Lab stepping in a hole or landing awkwardly when he jumps.

Broken toenails are another foot injury common to Labs. However, by keeping his toenails trimmed, you help reduce this risk. If he does break a toenail, he will bleed a lot. Remain calm and stop the bleeding by wrapping the foot in a towel or cloth and applying pressure to the broken nail. If the toenail break is not a clean one, the vet may have to surgically trim it, but the toenail will grow back.

CUTS AND SCRAPES

Your active Lab will no doubt get a cut or two throughout his life. Provided they are not deep enough to require stitches, you can clean cuts and scrapes with a sterile gauze pad and hydrogen peroxide. Once the wound is clean, apply an antibi-otic ointment, such as Polysporin, to help facilitate the healing process. If the cut shows signs of infection, such as swelling, redness, or tenderness, contact your vet.

FOXTAILS

If you spend any amount of time hik-ing or camping with your Lab, you will often have to remove foxtails from his body. Foxtails are dry, grassy heads surrounded by tiny, sharp spikes, which can become lodged in your Lab's fur, paws, and even in his ears, nose, and eyes. A foxtail in your Lab's eye will cause the eye socket to look glued shut.

If the foxtails are able to get into your dog's body, they can wreak havoc by causing infections. They could potentially kill your Lab if they are able to get into his spinal cord, lungs, heart, or brain.

Following each excursion, inspect your Lab's entire body, including between the toes, for foxtails. Remove any that you find. Softening the foxtails with a lubricant like mineral oil, vegetable oil, or baby oil will make them easier to remove.

KEEPING YOUR LAB ACTIVE

Although your Lab may not be as hyperactive as he was when he was a puppy, you still need to give him a lot of exercise. No matter the age, an under-exercised and bored Lab can be destructive.

Between six months and two years of age, your Labrador Retriever requires a minimum of two 30-minute walks or romps in the park every day. He won't care if it's snowing, raining, or blisteringly hot—he will need to get out there and burn off some energy.

While your young Lab will want to go non-stop, it is important that you don't overexert him, as this could be detrimental to his health. Keep in mind that your Lab's growth plates may not close until he's about 14 months old. Until this time, limit his jumping for Frisbees and tennis balls as this can put a lot of strain on his still-developing bones, ligaments, and overall musculoskeletal system, which can lead to fragile bones in your adult Lab. This does not mean

You don't have to limit your growing Labrador Retriever to walks around the block. He will enjoy participating in almost any outdoor activity you are doing, and will benefit from the exercise.

you can't play fetch with him—you just need to throw the balls low to the ground.

WHAT DO I FEED MY LAB?

Your puppy should remain on his large-breed puppy food until he is about 12 months old, at which time you should switch him over to a food specifically formulated for large breed adult dogs.

It is imperative that your Lab always be fed a high-quality food made for large breeds, as the ingredients—particularly the vitamins and minerals—will be in proper proportion to help slow his growth. If a large-breed dog, like a Lab, is fed a generic food, there is a possibility that he will develop skeletal complications such as hip and elbow dysplasia because the food contains too much fat. Too much fat leads to rapid growth in large-breed dogs. By feeding your Lab a high quality large-breed food, while providing him with a lot of exercise and limited treats, you will find it

Remember, dogs can't perspire to keep their bodies cool, so they become dehydrated more easily than humans do. Make sure fresh water is always available for your Lab.

easy to keep him at a healthy weight, which also helps to slow down his growth. This will help prevent your Lab from getting the degenerative joint disease osteochondrosis.

You may think that you are stunting your Lab's growth by feeding a large-breed food, but you aren't, you're just keeping it in check. He will eventually grow to his full height, weight, and size; it will just take a bit longer.

A Labrador Retriever that is nearly an adult shouldn't still be eating like a puppy. Find a large-breed food that is right for him.

SOCIALIZING A PEOPLE-ORIENTED DOG

If your neighbors didn't know who you were before you got your puppy, they will now. Labs are social ambassadors; they always want to meet everyone and be a part of whatever activity is going on, whether they are invited or not.

Keep in mind that between six months and two years of age your dog is in the midst of his teen years. Needless to say he is in conflict—he desperately wants to please you, but he will also knowingly defy you. During this phase, you will find yourself retraining him on the basic commands he once knew so well.

TRAINING

If for some reason you have so far avoided puppy school, you are at a critical juncture in you and your Lab's relationship: he is trying to overthrow your top dog position in the family so he can claim it for his

It is important to introduce your Labrador Retriever to new people, and train him not to react aggressively or inappropriately when he is out in public.

own. Obedience training can no longer be avoided.

A basic obedience class will use positive reinforcement techniques to teach you how to train your dog to "sit," "down," "stay," "come," and "heel." It will also help to socialize your dog with other people and dogs.

Ideally, you should begin teaching your puppy basic commands—"sit," "stay," "down"—when he is eight to ten weeks old. When your lab reaches his teen years, he will be more defiant and harder to teach, especially if you've never previously requested he

do as you say. But don't give up. He will quickly come around, provided you remain steadfast in what you want from him. Remember, training is about teaching your Lab to do what you want, when you want him to do it.

TRAVELING WITH YOUR LAB

Bringing your dog on out-of-town trips puts new meaning to the phrase "family vacation." But each year more and more people decide to bring their dogs with them on vacation. In order to have a fun and

Bringing your Labrador Retriever along on vacation means extra work, but it can also be great fun.

relaxing time with your Lab, you have to careully plan your destination, route, mode of transportation, and accommodations.

With the exception of guide dogs, trains and buses do not allow dogs on board, but some airlines do. If you're going to travel by plane, you have to first find out if the airline will accept your Lab. Some airlines are no longer accepting large dogs, even in the cargo hold, where they have traditionally traveled on the plane.

If you are flying into another country, find out if he will even be allowed into the country without having to be quarantined for a significant period of time. You will need to ensure you have all of his vaccines up-to-date, as well as have any necessary paperwork on hand.

FAST FACT

In the event of an accident in a car traveling only 30 mph, an unrestrained 50-pound dog would be thrown with great force—equivalent to nine 168-pound men, according to statistics from the SPCA.

When people vacation with their dogs, they typically travel by car. Driving to your destination enables you to stop as many times as necessary so your dog has ample opportunities to relieve himself and stretch his legs.

Always ensure that your Labrador Retriever is securely fastened. This can be with a dog seatbelt, in his crate, or behind a vehicle barrier.

CANINE CAR SAFETY

Dogs should never be left alone in a vehicle, especially in the summer. The car's temperature can quickly rise, causing your Lab to suffer a heatstroke. If this occurs and he is not given immediate medical attention, death is likely.

These precautions are not only necessary to ensure your dog's safety, they also enable you to focus on driving, rather than fending off an 80-pound Lab who wants to curl up on your lap.

Once you know where you are going and how you're getting there, you need to consider your accommodations. Not every hotel or motel accepts pets, so before you get in your car and decide to head out on the open road, you need to plan your overnight stays.

When booking your room, make sure to inquire about the establishment's pet policy. Some pet-friendly hotels or motels will only allow one small dog or cat (or just cats) in their rooms. You may also be charged an extra fee. Before booking the room, ask what the fee is and whether it's refundable.

Don't forget to pack a bag for your Lab. In his bag you should pack food, bowls, toys, treats, medications, a first aid kit, and travel documents. You also need to bring a blanket or bed, collar with identification tags, and leash. It's a good idea to bring carpet cleaner, because you never know if all this traveling is going to stress him out and cause him to have an accident or an upset stomach. You may also want to bring a couple of old sheets to throw over the hotel furniture because you know your Lab

is going to make himself at home when you stop for the night.

For some people, vacationing with their Lab does not sound like much of a relaxing time, so there are pet care alternatives available.

One option is to have a friend or family member stay at your house while you're away. This causes the least amount of disruption to your dog, and knowing that someone you know is watching your dog will comfort you. The person you choose for your dog should have a similar schedule as you and be willing to do everything associated with caring for your Lab, which includes feeding him on schedule and giving him an adequate amount of regular exercise.

If you don't know anyone who can do this, there are professional pet sitting companies that provide this service. Before you hire anyone, interview them and pay close attention to how the pet sitter and your

FAST FACT

Boston's Fairmont Copley Plaza Hotel has a black Lab named Catie Copley as a canine ambassador. Catie was originally trained as a guide dog, but can now be found being walked around the city by the hotel's guests.

dog get along. When interviewing the pet sitter, ask him or her for references and whether or not he or she is bonded and insured.

Whether you have a friend, family member, or professional pet sitter staying at your home to care for your Lab, make sure you leave that person with all the details of your dog's eating habits:

- his feeding schedule, which includes the amount of food he gets per meal and at what time;
- where the food is located;
- the brand of food, just in case she needs to buy more while you are away.

You also need to provide information on any medication your dog is on, including dosage and administration instructions.

You will also want to provide the caretaker with information about your Lab's daily exercise requirements—the times he generally goes for a walk or to the park, and the walking route and/or park location.

If you don't want anyone staying at your home, you can always send your dog to a boarding facility. Many professional pet care people open their homes to other dogs. While there, your dog becomes a family's guest. Only one or two dogs are allowed at one time.

Kennels are another option. They typically house the dog in a large, no-frills room that has access to an outdoor run. There is generally minimal contact with other people and dogs.

There are also 24-hour doggy day cares. These facilities run a doggy day care during the day, which provides your Lab with a lot of new friends and playtime. At night, the day care is turned into one giant bedroom where the dogs snore the night away. These types of facilities will have a staff member on site to supervise the dogs throughout the night.

Prices vary for each of the services mentioned. Make sure you check what the pick up and drop off times

The Web site of the National Association of Professional Pet Sitters, www.petsitters.org, can be used to help you find the right person to watch your pet while you're away.

and policies are, where applicable, as well as what their emergency procedures are, just in case your dog becomes injured while in their care. And you must provide them with contact information for someone other than yourself who is authorized to act on your behalf, just in case you cannot be reached in case of emergency.

CHAPTER SEVEN

Things to Do With Your Adult Lab

The Labrador Retriever was initially bred to work alongside fishermen and hunters. But over the years, the Lab's role in society has changed and he is now North America's number one canine companion. However, although the Lab's skills may no longer be required to help feed a village, they are still in demand.

SERVICE DOGS

Service dogs are specially trained to help people with disabilities, particularly those who are blind or hearing impaired, live independently. A service

Labs make great service dogs, as they can be trained to guide blind owners through busy streets.

dog is taught over 80 commands that include retrieving keys, television remotes, and telephones; opening refrigerators and bringing food (without eating it) to his owner; pushing elevator buttons; turning lights on and off; opening doors; alerting his owner that the doorbell or telephone is ringing or that the smoke alarm or alarm clock is going off; and alerting the owner to crossing traffic.

Perhaps just as important as their skills, these specially trained Labs also provide companionship. The Lab's easygoing personality is what has made him a popular assistance and service dog. The Lab makes a great service dog because he easily adapts to whatever situation he is in—from a busy urban center's public transportation system, to a quiet restaurant, to sitting by his owner's side at home.

Not every Lab will make a good service dog. A service dog must have a high retrieval drive, as he will be required to retrieve a lot of items. He must also have the right temperament, as well as a strong desire to work, and a high level of concentration while at work. He must also take initiative yet have a strong need to please. He must be calm and quiet, and not too dominant or too submissive. Because of their specialized temperament, some breeders breed only service dogs to ensure their quality.

Service training for these dogs starts when they are eight weeks old. While living in a volunteer family's home for the first 12 to 18 months of his life, he will live, learn, and act like other Labs, but when he is about a year and a half, he will leave the family and either go back to the breeder or go to a special training center, where he will be reevaluated for the service dog program. If he is still a good candidate for the program, he is then taught all of the skills needed to help a person requiring his assistance.

SEARCH AND RESCUE

The Lab's natural scenting abilities, retrieving skills, endurance, and desire to work alongside people make these dogs great for search and rescue missions. Search-and-rescue (SAR) dogs are trained by the National

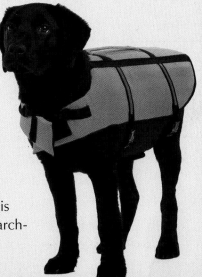

The Labrador Retriever's skill at tracking makes this breed ideal as search-and-rescue dogs.

Association for Search and Rescue to find lost or missing people who are either alive or dead. This is done in two different ways. The first is by airborne scent. The SAR dog follows the missing person's smell through the air. The other method is trailing. A piece of clothing from the missing person is provided for the dog to smell; he then follows that specific scent.

SAR dogs can be specially trained for different situations such as avalanche, disaster, water, wilderness, and urban searches.

DETECTION AND POLICE DOGS

During World War II, Labs were used to detect mines. Today, the FBI, the U.S. Customs department, and police and fire departments use detection dogs to sniff out explo-sives, narcotics, accelerants, weapons, toxic materials, and other illegal substances.

Accelerant dogs are used by fire departments to search a fire scene for the smallest traces of flammable liquid, such as gasoline and paint thinner, that may have been used to start the fire.

Dogs used by the FBI are trained to identify about 19,000 different combinations of explosive chemicals. This type of dog is trained to sit next to the contraband or accelerant, which alerts the handler that he has found something. The dog is then rewarded with a tennis ball and the knowledge that he did his job.

THERAPY DOG

A visit from a dog while a person lies in a hospital bed can do wonders for his or her spirits and recovery. Therapy dogs provide companionship and comfort to people in hospitals, nursing homes, and rehabilitation facilities. Something as simple as petting a dog can lower a person's blood pressure, or help a withdrawn patient become more outgoing.

A therapy dog must be friendly and well mannered, which means he must enjoy meeting new people and accept being petted by a lot of strangers. Therapy dogs must also be able to handle crowds, and be comfortable around wheelchairs, walkers, and people on crutches. Knowing a trick or two like "paw" or "speak" doesn't hurt either.

If you are more interested in entering your dog in competitions than training him for service, there are many options available.

THE DOG SHOW CIRCUIT

Conformation shows are all about finding dogs that most closely replicate the breed standard. These shows are for purebred dogs only, as the contestants—particularly the win-

ners—become highly coveted breeding stock. Labs can be disqualified from competition if they are taller or shorter than the AKC standard stipulates; the dog has a pink nose or his/her nose has no color at all; the eye rims are not dark; the Lab's tail has been docked (shortened); or the Lab is not black, chocolate or yellow.

Dogs in the show ring vie for points towards their championship title. A maximum of five points can be earned per show and a total of 15 points, from various judges, is required for a Lab to be called a

Showing a dog involves a lot of hard work and preparation, but many people find it emotionally rewarding.

champion. This designation will enable you to put "Ch" before his name. Conformation focuses on how the dog physically compares to the standard, but a championship Lab must also have a lot of personality, expression, and showmanship.

Before you enter your first show, attend one to get a backstage view of the process. You'll see that the dogs and owners have done a lot of training and preparation.

If this is still something you'd like to do, you'll want to find a conformation training class in your area. (Your breeder may be able to help with your search.) The classes will teach you how to stack your Lab (show off his outline), walk him through the rings, and groom him properly. When your Lab is three months old, he can

join the training classes; however, he won't be able to enter a show until he is six months old.

Labs are very easy to groom for shows—bathe him a day or two before the show, trim his nails, and you're done.

When in the ring, a judge will examine each dog's face—eyes, teeth, ears, and bite—and she will feel the dog's hind and forelegs for structure. The judge will also feel a male dog's testicles to ensure they are fully descended, and to confirm that the Lab is intact (spayed or neutered dogs cannot participate in conformation shows).

Showing your dog takes a lot of work. If your Lab enjoys shows but you find them too time-consuming, consider hiring a professional handler. Look for a handler who has experience with the breed, and knows how to motivate, condition, and reward a Lab. You also want a handler who will make your dog a priority, so you need to know how many other dogs the handler is working with and how much attention your dog will get. Hiring a professional is expensive, so make sure you get your money's worth.

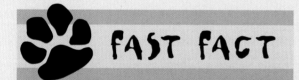

FAST FACT

A working Lab, whether in the field, show ring, or on the agility course, requires a diet that is high in protein and fat. This diet will enable him to maintain his muscle mass and keep his weight stable. However, be careful not to overfeed your Lab. No matter how much he works, he won't be able to burn off all of the extra fat and calories. Your Lab can't perform well if he becomes obese.

OBEDIENCE COMPETITION

If you have a very well-behaved Lab, why not show him off while trying to

SPECIALTY SHOWS

There are three types of conformation shows—specialty, group, and all-breed.

Specialty show competitors are all from one breed of dog. Labrador Retriever breeders typically judge these shows, as they are experts in all things Lab. There are three levels of specialty shows—local, regional, and national.

Within the specialty show, there are various sub-groups, such as veteran (dogs 10 years and older) or puppy (three to six months old). There are also bitch and stud dog categories, which are for the offspring of dogs entered in the competition.

Group shows are for dogs that belong to a specific group. For example, Labrador Retrievers belong to the sporting group, so they compete against all of the other breeds within the sporting group for top honors.

All-breed shows pit different breeds against each other for the title "Best in Show." Perhaps the most famous of these is the annual Westminster Kennel Club show.

win an obedience competition or two? Obedience competitions involve more than proving that your Lab can "sit," "down," "stay," "come," and "heel." You must show that your Lab is capable of doing all those things while surrounded by any number of people and dogs.

If you want your Lab to be titled, be sure to enter AKC-sanctioned obedience competitions. Obedience titles include Companion Dog (CD), Companion Dog Excellent (CDX), both in the novice class, and Utility Dog (UD). For dogs that have succeeded in obtaining their CD, CDX and UD titles, you can progress to the advanced titles—Utility Dog

Excellent (UDX) and Obedience Trial Champion (OTCh). In order to progress through the levels, however, your Lab must earn at least 170 points out of a possible 200 by completing certain exercises.

Unlike conformation competitions that focus a lot of attention on appearance, obedience trials focus less on appearance and more on skill. But a well-groomed Lab is still imperative.

Spayed and neutered dogs are able to participate in obedience trials, as are dogs that have had surgery to repair an inherited defect. However, your Lab may not participate in obedience competitions if he or she is under six months old, is a female in heat, is visually or hearing impaired, is lame, or has a medical device attached to his or her body.

TRACKING

Tracking tests your Lab's ability to track a scent. Labs are not scent hounds, but they do have an excellent sense of smell and do very well in this event.

Tracking is very complex and requires a lot of specialized training. To be a tracker, your Lab must also be proficient in obedience, which is why a lot of people tackle tracking once they've exhausted the obedience circuit.

To test your Lab's scent skill, try this exercise: show your Lab an article of clothing, such as a glove or hat. Tease him with it and make it something he would want to find. You can even put treats in it to encourage his interest in the item.

Once you've got him interested, put your Lab into a sit-stay and walk away from him in a straight line. You want to go about 10 feet away. Walk back to your Lab and tell him to "find" the object. If he's associated the hat or glove with being a toy, he will immediately race to grab the item and bring it back to you. When he brings it back, give him a lot of praise.

If your dog didn't stay while you walked away or did not go for the item, it does not mean your Lab won't be successful at tracking, it just means you have a bit of work ahead of you.

Titles your Lab can earn in tracking are Tracking Dog (TD), Tracking Dog Excellent (TDX), and Variable Surface Tracking Test (VST). If your Lab successfully obtains all three titles, he will automatically earn his Champion Tracker (CT) title.

FIELD TRIALS

Being the hunters they are, Labs excel in hunt tests and field trials, which test a Lab's ability to retrieve game. A good retriever will perform well in water and on land, pay attention to his handler, and won't shy away from the sound of gunfire or damage the bird when he carries it back to the handler.

Just as conformation shows determine the quality of Lab for breeding stock, so do field tests when it comes to hunting Labs. Therefore, no spayed or neutered Labs are able to compete in field trials. Competitors must also be at least six months old and registered with the AKC.

A Lab can earn the title of Field Champion (FC) or Amateur Field Champion (AFC), which can become part of the dog's name upon winning.

Field trials are divided into two classes, each of which test Labs of

In a Tracking competition, the owner must tell her dog to "find" an object. This Lab has willingly returned the dummy to his owner, which would mean a higher score.

various ages, levels and experience. There are also separate categories for amateur and professional handlers.

Field trials have four classes—two major (open all age and amateur all age) and two minor (qualifying and derby). Championship points are awarded only in the major classes.

Dogs are judged on their natural skills (attention, courage, intelligence, memory, perseverance, and style) as well as on skills that require a lot of training (control, delivery, response to direction, and steadiness).

A Lab will be eliminated from competition if he fails to enter unpleasant conditions and difficult situations such as rough cover, mud, ice, or water. He will also be disqualified if he returns to the handler before finding the bird in a marked retrieve (he sees where the bird lands), stops hunting for the fallen bird, has an obvious poor scenting ability, or if he fails to pick up the bird once he finds it.

HUNT TESTS

Hunt tests judge a Lab's ability to work as a retriever and hunting companion in the field. However, instead of competing against other dogs, like in field trials, Labs competing in hunt tests are judged against a performance standard that is laid out by the AKC.

Hunt tests also differ from field trials in that a Lab that has no AKC registration papers, but is recognized as a purebred, is allowed to participate. A dog like this has what is called indefinite listing privilege (ILP).

While a hunt test is not a competition, Labs can earn various hunt test titles: Junior Hunter (JH), Senior Hunter (SH), and Master Hunter (MH).

Dogs are judged on marking (his ability to watch and recall where the bird landed so he is able to retrieve it) and style (how he acts, his alertness, eagerness, and quickness to retrieve). The Lab is also judged on how he enters the water and picks up the bird, as well as his perseverance and courage (he cannot show any fear or lack of confidence); trainability (not as important as his natural retrieving abilities, but he must be able to stay on the line without fidgeting); how responsive

Labrador Retrievers were bred for hunting, so with a little training they can excel at hunt tests.

Agility courses can provide a fun challenge for your Lab.

he is to all requests and direction; and how he delivers the bird (he must willingly bring it to the handler without dropping it).

As with field trial training, look for classes through your local hunt and retriever clubs.

AGILITY

Agility has become one of the most popular dog sports in North America. Why? Because it's a lot of fun and a great way to keep your Lab in shape, while reinforcing and adding new skills to his obedience repertoire.

What is agility? It's an obstacle course in which your Lab, helped by verbal assistance from his handler, must maneuver over balance beams, through tunnels, and around poles as well as jump through tires and hoops and over bars.

The dog is judged on his time and accuracy. Prior to the start of the event, judges determine the set course time, and the dog is penalized if he takes any longer than that.

Mixed breeds and AKC registered dogs are both eligible to compete.

Before you sign up for your first agility class, your Lab has to know the basic commands, which include "sit," "down," "stay," and "come." You should also get clearance from your veterinarian, as agility can be hard on a dog's body.

You should also have realistic expectations. Labs are athletic and smart, but they are not going to be the quickest and best at agility. (That honor typically goes to the Border Collie). But your Lab will do well and always put on a good show— even when he gets distracted in the middle of the course by a bird flying past that becomes more interesting then completing the course.

FLYBALL

Agility isn't the only dog sport. Flyball and Frisbee are fun for Labs, too—especially those dogs that can retrieve things with real flair.

Flyball is a team sport, with the objective being that each of the four dogs on the team must jump over hurdles on their way to the flyball box. Once at the box, the dog must step on a lever that triggers a tennis ball to be released. With the ball in his mouth, the dog goes back to the starting line, by jumping over the hurdles again. The first team to cross the finish line mistake-free— no toppled or missed hurdles—wins.

Labs love flyball, as it satisfies their natural instinct to retrieve and their obsession with tennis balls. However, flyball is very hard on a Lab's body, especially the elbows, knees, shoulders, and hocks. Before signing up for a flyball class, book an appointment with your veterinarian that includes getting your Lab's joints x-rayed.

A growing dog sport that Labs thrive in is Frisbee competitions. A competition will generally consist of two parts: a freestyle portion that focuses on athleticism, presentation, and the "How cool is that?!" factor. The second part of the competition is focused on distance, accuracy, and precision.

While these are great physical and mental activities, you have to ensure they are not the only physical activity your Lab gets. You still need to have him do all things Lab—take walks, go for romps in the park, and swim in the lake.

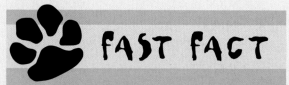

FAST FACT

Avoid doing a lot of box work and hurdle jumping when training your young Lab for flyball. His growth plates may not close until he is around 14 months old. Until then, he should only be jumping low hurdles.

With a little practice, your Lab will be able to catch a Frisbee with style.

FREESTYLE

Freestyle is all about showcasing the relationship you have with your Lab through a routine set to music.

Routines are based on your dog's obedience skills, tricks, or anything else he excels at. These are incorporated into either a heelwork routine (dog must heel on all sides of the handler no more than four feet apart from each other) or a musical freestyle routine, where anything goes.

Freestyle competitions, which are organized by the Canine Freestyle Federation, are open to all AKC registered and unregistered Labs, as well as to dogs that have been spayed or neutered. Labs with health issues are even able to participate.

CANINE GOOD CITIZEN TEST

The foundation for any canine job is the Canine Good Citizen (CGC) test. The CGC, which was implemented in 1989 by the AKC, is a non-competitive, one-time, pass or fail test that consists of 10 elements. The purpose of the CGC is to recognize dogs with great manners. Although the AKC designed the test, all dogs—whether purebred or mixed breed—can earn the CGC title. The 10 areas tested are as follows:

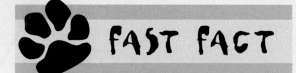

FAST FACT

The International Disc Dog Handlers Association holds a Retrieval Proficiency Test (RPT), which measures a dog's ability to retrieve virtually any object.

The RPT consists of the handler throwing an object a distance that is at least equal to two lengths of your Lab. Using only verbal requests—no corrections are allowed—and hand signals, your Lab must go pick up the object and bring it back. Your dog passes the test if he is able to complete the retrieve in a time frame that is less than the time it would have taken for you to walk up to the object, pick it up, and bring it back to the spot from which it was thrown. You get one practice throw, and then the test is conducted.

ACCEPTING A FRIENDLY STRANGER: Your Lab must remain well behaved, showing no fear, shyness, or guarding, when a stranger approaches and shakes your hand.

SITTING POLITELY FOR PETTING: While sitting beside you, your Lab must be willing to accept being petted and touched by a stranger.

APPEARANCE AND GROOMING: Your Lab must allow a stranger to brush him, pick up each foot for examination, and check inside his ears. He cannot show any signs of aggression or shyness.

WALK ON A LOOSE LEASH: Your dog must walk beside you on a loose leash while making turns and stops.

WALK THROUGH A CROWD: Your Lab must remain calm while walking through a crowd of people. He is allowed to show interest in the people, but he cannot jump, pull, or act fearful.

SIT AND DOWN ON COMMAND— STAY IN PLACE: Your dog must sit and lie down when you give him the commands to do so. You are allowed to give your Lab the command more than once and use more than one word—a phrase is acceptable. He must then remain in the sit or down position while you walk 20 feet away and then back to your dog.

COME WHEN CALLED: With your dog in a stay, or with the evaluator distracting your Lab by petting him, walk 10 feet away from your Lab, then call him to come. He must come to you.

REACTION TO ANOTHER DOG: You and your dog will walk up to another person and her dog. You will stop, shake hands, and have a brief conversation. During this time, your Lab should show no more than a passing interest in the other dog. You and your dog then walk away. Neither dog can show shyness or aggression.

REACTION TO DISTRACTION: During simulated everyday situations, your Lab must remain calm.

He can show a natural curiosity and be a little startled, but he cannot show aggression, panic, or fear.

SUPERVISED SEPARATION: Your Lab proves that he can be well behaved when left alone for three minutes with another person.

CHAPTER EIGHT

The Golden Years

Nobody likes to get older, but it's a fact of life that can't be avoided. Unfortunately, dogs have much shorter life spans than humans—one year for a human is equal to seven years in a dog's lifespan. This means when your Lab is seven years old, he's middle-aged—the equivalent of a 49-year-old human. This is also about the same time in your Lab's life when he will start graying around the muzzle. He'll have less energy and may experience vision and hearing loss.

Despite a slowdown in energy and an increased potential for debilitating diseases, an older Lab can still be an absolute joy to be around. The crazy puppy days, terrible twos, and adolescent phases are gone and

Going a little gray and having less energy as they age is natural for Labs, just as it is for humans.

replaced with a confident, well-mannered Lab that just wants to hang out with you and enjoy life.

HEALTH PROBLEMS

A Lab is defined as a senior when he is seven or eight years old. It is at this age that his annual exam with the veterinarian should also include a geriatric screening, which will establish a baseline for later comparison. It will consist of a myriad of tests to determine how your Lab's internal organs are functioning, and check your Lab's teeth, eyesight, joint mobility, and weight.

Depending on the health of your senior Lab, your veterinarian may recommend regular visits be made every six months instead of annually.

Age-related health issues are inevitable, despite your best efforts to avoid them by providing your Lab with exceptional veterinary care. An aging Lab may one day suffer from various conditions, including arthritis, diabetes, cognitive dysfunction syndrome, hearing and vision loss, hypothyroidism, laryngeal paralysis, and kidney disease.

ARTHRITIS

There is no cure for arthritis, which is a degenerative joint disease, but there are many supplements and medications available to help ease

FAST FACT

Dogs, like people, age differently. Some dogs will show signs of aging at a relatively young age, while some Labs will continue acting like a puppy until they are 12 or 15 years old.

the pain and slow progression of the disease.

As dogs get older, they naturally slow down, so you may not initially recognize the onset of arthritis. Watch for symptoms of arthritis, which include decreased activity level; a reluctance to climb stairs; an unwillingness to get into the car; stiffness when he wakes up from a nap; and swollen joints. When you try to touch a dog with arthritis in the joint areas, they will feel tender and hot. He may even snap at you when you touch them because they are so painful.

There are numerous things you can do to help alleviate the pain of arthritis. The most important is weight management. If a Lab is carrying around extra weight, it puts a lot of stress and strain on his joints, which magnifies the arthritic pain. If your Lab is overweight, having him drop just a few pounds will go a long way toward relieving his joint pain.

Your older Labrador Retriever's health and strength might not be what they once were, but he's still your friend and you can have a great time together during his later years.

There are numerous medications and supplements also available to help relieve the pain. Your vet may prescribe an anti-inflammatory medication for your Lab. These anti-inflammatories can be very effective for most Labs, but they do come with potential side effects, from diarrhea and vomiting to potential kidney or liver damage. If you and your veterinarian decide to use anti-inflammatories for your Lab over an extended period of time, make sure to get regular liver and kidney function tests.

Supplements do not provide immediate pain relief—they take about six weeks to take effect—but they are believed to help restore joint function and reduce pain with virtually no negative side effects. The most common supplements used for arthritis are glucosamine and chondroitin. Other supplements also deemed beneficial are Ester C and MSM.

While such drugs as acetaminophen or ibuprofen may work for humans, never give them to your Lab. They can be toxic to dogs.

DIABETES

Diabetes, like arthritis, is common in older Labs. It has no known cure, but can be managed quite effectively.

In a non-diabetic dog the pancreas will produce insulin, which the body uses to regulate the amount of glucose (sugar) in the bloodstream. In a diabetic dog, the pancreas fails to produce a sufficient amount of insulin for his body, or the pancreas may fail to produce the insulin all together, causing the dog's glucose levels to spike and cause the dog to feel very sick. Symptoms include excessive thirst and urination.

Blood and urinalysis tests conducted by your veterinarian are required to correctly diagnose diabetes.

The disease can be managed by giving your Lab daily insulin shots.

COGNITIVE DYSFUNCTION SYNDROME (CDS)

As dogs get older, they tend to become forgetful and withdrawn from the family, as well as less active and more likely to fall asleep. Your Lab may even start having accidents in the house. While there is no known medical reason for these occurrences, they are simply deemed age-related and called cognitive dysfunction syndrome (CDS).

There is no cure for CDS, but medications are available that may be helpful in restoring your dog's cognitive function.

HEARING AND VISION LOSS

When your Lab was younger, you might have thought he was deaf because he would not listen to you. But as he gets older, he may actually be losing his hearing. Canine deafness is usually caused by a neurological deterioration of the dog's inner ear. It can occur to one or both ears

Erratic behavior and constant exhaustion could be signs of cognitive dysfunction syndrome, a problem that affects many older dogs.

and it usually results in a progressive loss of hearing.

Cataracts often affect older Labs and Labs suffering from diabetes, which causes them to lose their vision.

Your Lab may have cloudy eyes but not be suffering from cataracts. The cloudy lens is called nucleus sclerosis, which occurs as part of a Lab's natural aging process. It is caused by the fibers that form around the edge of the eye's lens. The fibers then push toward the center of the eye. Nucleus sclerosis does not usually cause blindness, but it will make it difficult for your Lab to focus on close-up objects.

Labs have great memories, so despite losing their vision, as long as

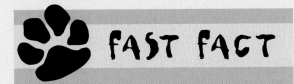

FAST FACT

Talk to your vet before concluding your Lab suffers from CDS, as some of these symptoms can also be signs of problems with the adrenal gland, thyroid, or kidneys.

you don't move or rearrange your furniture, he will be able to move around the house on his own quite well.

HYPOTHYROIDISM

Hypothyroidism occurs when the thyroid hormone is below its optimal level, causing many of the dog's organs to malfunction.

Symptoms of hypothyroidism include weight gain, hair loss, dry and itchy skin, chronic ear infections, and allergic reactions.

Hypothyroidism is tested via blood work and can be managed with daily medication.

LARYNGEAL PARALYSIS (LP)

Laryngeal paralysis (LP) occurs when the Lab's voice box (larynx) fails to open properly when the dog inhales, causing an airway obstruction. There is no known cause for the condition, but it can be the result of an injured larynx or laryngeal nerves.

How do you know your Lab may be suffering from LP? Your Lab will have a difficult time breathing and will do so quite noisily, he will gag or cough when he eats or drinks, and he will have bluish-colored gums and no energy.

LP is diagnosed through a physical exam, which includes checking the dog's larynx as well as taking chest x-rays.

If your Lab is diagnosed with LP, a mild case can be easily treated by adjusting some of his daily activities, such as having him avoid stressful situations; limiting his activities, especially on hot days; and controlling his weight. You may also opt to walk your Lab on a harness instead of a neck collar to avoid putting more pressure on the larynx area.

If it is a severe case of LP, your vet may recommend removing the portion of his larynx that is creating the obstructed airflow.

KIDNEY DISEASE

Kidneys are vital to the body as they remove waste from it and enable the body's organs to maintain appropriate vitamin, mineral and water levels.

Symptoms of kidney disease include increased thirst and urination, but because these are also symptoms for other diseases, blood tests must be conducted to determine the kidneys' functionality. This should be part of your Lab's geriatric exam.

NUTRITION FOR THE SENIOR LAB

As your Lab gets older, his nutritional needs will change. That does not mean that as soon as he turns seven or eight years old you need to put him on a "senior" diet. However, if you've noticed he is packing on the pounds, you may want to either feed him less of his current food, or switch him to a senior food, especially if he is less active then before.

If you do decide to feed your Lab a food created for senior dogs, again, choose an all-natural premium brand. The company that manufactures the adult food you currently feed your Lab may even have a senior formula.

When reading the label, make sure the food is high in protein—about 25 percent. The food should also be reduced in fat and calories (when compared to an adult maintenance food) and be high in fiber.

Even if your senior Lab is moving slower than when he was a puppy, he'll still want, and need, regular exercise.

AN OLD LAB IS STILL AN ACTIVE LAB

Just because your Lab has a graying muzzle and may not be as quick as he once was doesn't mean he's ready to watch the world go by from the front porch.

As long as your Lab doesn't have any medical issues that would preclude him from continuing to enjoy his regular activities, he should be allowed to do so. In fact, if you start

FAST FACT

Diabetes is most commonly found in female Labs between six and nine years of age, especially those who are overweight. A genetic predisposition to diabetes can be a contributing factor.

Swimming is a good way for an older Lab to exercise without overexerting himself, especially if he's arthritic.

taking away the romps in the park and shortening his walks, you will find that he may actually age more quickly.

If he loves the water (and really, what Lab doesn't?), you may want to take him to a lake or dog pool more often. Swimming provides great exercise for your Lab without stressing his aging joints. Swimming is also particularly good for the arthritic Lab.

SAYING GOODBYE

Hopefully you and your Lab have had a long, happy time together. You may have spent up to 15 years of your life with your Lab, so saying goodbye will be difficult.

Most people prefer to avoid thinking about ending their Lab's life, but it is very rare for a dog to die peacefully of old age in his sleep. In the case of illness that can't be cured, euthanasia may be the least painful option—both for you and for your dog.

You will know when it's time to say goodbye. At some point your Lab may be in so much physical pain from a debilitating or terminal disease that he can no longer enjoy even the simplest pleasures in life. By prolonging the inevitable, you actually cause him to suffer even more.

Euthanasia is painless to the dog. The veterinarian injects your Lab

"mommy, WHERE'S BUDDy?"

If there are children in your family, don't sugarcoat the death of their beloved Lab. Be honest in explaining to them what has happened—whether he died as a result of a car accident or whether he has finally succumbed to a debilitating disease such as cancer.

This may be your child's first experience with death, so you need to be careful about what words you use to describe death. Avoid using the word "sleep" when describing death to a young child. Your child may all of a sudden develop a fear of sleeping because he or she does not want to die.

with a drug that slows down his heart and causes him to die.

It will be normal for you to feel the loss of your constant companion and it is just as important that you don't ignore those feelings. Friends and other family members who understand your bond will be there for you—lean on them in this time of sorrow.

If your Lab was one of numerous dogs living in your home, you may find that the remaining dogs will go through their own grieving process. They may not eat or drink and start to mope around the house. That's okay, as it's all part of their grieving process.

A NEW LAB

Wait a while before bringing another Lab into your life. You need time to properly grieve and make peace with the passing of this Lab before bringing a new one home. If you bring a

new dog into your home too soon, you won't be able to form a unique and wonderful bond with the new Lab as you will be too consumed with the old relationship you are actually trying to replicate.

When your Labrador Retriever passes away, give yourself time to grieve and come to terms with your loss. Remember the good times.

Organizations to Contact

**American Animal
Hospital Association**
12575 West Bayaud Ave.
Lakewood, CO 80228
Phone: 303-986-2800
Fax: 800-252-2242
Email: info@aahanet.org
Web site: www.aahanet.org

American Kennel Club
260 Madison Ave
New York, NY 10016
Phone: 212-696-8200
Web site: www.akc.org

Association of Pet Dog Trainers
150 Executive Center Drive, Box 35
Greenville, SC 29615
Phone: 1-800-738-3647
Fax: 1-864-331-0767
Email: information@apdt.com
Web site: www.apdt.com

The Canadian Kennel Club
89 Skyway Avenue, Suite 100
Etobicoke, Ontario
M9W 6R4 Canada
Phone: 416-675-5511
Fax: 416-675-6506
Email: information@ckc.ca
Web site: www.ckc.ca

**Canine Eye Registration
Foundation**
1717 Philo Road
P.O. Box 3007
Urbana, IL 61803-3007
Phone: 217-693-4800
Fax: 217-693-4801
Email: CERF@vmdb.org
Web site: www.vmdb.org

**The Kennel Club of
the United Kingdom**
1-5 Clarges Street
Piccadilly, London
W1J 8AB
United Kingdom
Phone: 0870-606-6750
Fax: 020-7518-1058
Web site: www.thekennelclub.org.uk

The Labrador Retriever Club
Cheri Conway, membership
chairman
24670 Schaupp Road
Klamath Falls, OR 97603
Phone: 541-723-2467
Email: info@thelabradorclub.com
Web site: www.thelabradorclub.com

LABMED Inc.
3941 Legacy Drive, Suite 204,
#A115
Plano, TX 75023
Phone: 972-208-2470
Fax: 972-692-8300
Email: info@labmed.org
Web site: www.labmed.org

**National Association of
Dog Obedience Instructors**
PMB 369
729 Grapevine Hwy
Hurst, TX 76054-2085
Email: corrsec2@nadoi.org
Web site: www.nadoi.org

National Dog Registry
P.O. Box 51105
Mesa, AZ 85208
Phone: 800-NDR-DOGS
Email: info@nationaldogregistry.com
Web site: www.nationaldogregistry.com

Pet Sitters International
418 East King Street
King, NC 27021-9163
Phone: 336-983-9222
Fax: 336-983-3755
Web site: www.petsit.com

UK National Pet Register
74 North Albert Street, Dept 2
Fleetwood, Lancashire
FY7 6BJ
United Kingdom
Web site: www.nationalpetregister.org

Further Reading

Brown, Andi. *Whole Pet Diet: Eight Weeks to Great Health for Dogs And Cats.* Berkeley, Calif.: Celestial Arts, 2006.

Eldredge, Debra, and Kim Campbell Thornton. *Everything Dog Health Book: A Complete Guide To Keeping Your Best Friend Healthy From Head To Tail.* Cincinnati: Adams Media, 2005.

Guthrie, Sue, Dick Lane, and G. Sumner-Smith. *The Guide Dogs Book of Ultimate Dog Care.* Gloucestershire, United Kingdom: Ringpress Books, 2004.

Hodgson, Sarah. *Puppies For Dummies.* 2nd edition. Indianapolis: Wiley Publishing, 2006.

Milner, Robert. *Retriever Training: A Back-to-Basics Approach.* Memphis: Ducks Unlimited, 2005.

Pitcairn, Richard H., and Susan Hubble Pitcairn. *Dr. Pitcairn's New Complete Guide to Natural Health for Dogs and Cats.* New York: Rodale Books, 2005.

Rutherford, Clarice, and David H. Neil. *How to Raise a Puppy You Can Live With.* 4th edition. Loveland, Colo.: Alpine Blue Ribbon Books, 2005.

Internet Resources

www.akc.org/breeds/labrador_retriever/index.cfm

> You will find the American Kennel Club's breed standard for the Labrador Retriever at this site.

www.canadasguidetodogs.com/retrieverlab.htm

> History, profile, and links to additional Lab organizations can be found through this site.

http://dogs.about.com/cs/breedprofiles/p/labrador.htm

> This site contains a short synopsis about the history, size, and temperament of Labrador Retrievers.

http://grreat.org/microchip.htm

> Everything you want to know about microchip-tagging your pet.

www.pamperedpuppy.com

> This Web site offers cute gifts for dogs, as well as links to informative articles.

www.veterinarypartner.com/Content.plx?P=A&A=2244

> Information on what makes the Lab such a good service dog.

Index

adolescence, 66–67, 69–70
  See also puppies
adoption, dog, 35, 42, 44–47
  See also ownership, dog
Agility dog sports, 99–100
  See also dog shows
American Animal Hospital Association
  (AAHA), 47
American Association of Food Controls
  Officials (AAFCO), 64
American Kennel Club (AKC), 9, 17, 18,
  19–23, 38, 57–58, 93, 95, 98
  and the Canine Good Citizen test,
    101–103
American Kennel Gazette, 17
anterior cruciate ligament (ACL) tears, 81
arthritis, 105–106

barking, 25, 29, 30, 36
bathing, 71–72
  See also grooming
behavior, 46
  See also training
biting, 31
  See also legal issues
bloat, 66
boarding, 39, 88–89
  See also traveling
bordetella, 62
breed history, 16–19, 21, 23
breed standards, 19–23, 93
breeders, 18, 41–42, 57–58
  choosing, 38–41
Buccleugh (Duke), 18

Canada, 16–17, 18, 20
Canadian Kennel Club, 9, 38
Canine Eye Registration Foundation

(CERF), 57, 58
  See also breeders
Canine Freestyle Federation, 101
Canine Good Citizen test, 101–103
canine hepatitis, 62
car safety, 86–87
  See also traveling
cataracts, 107
Catie Copley (Labrador Retriever), 87
Center for Disease Control, 31
certification, 57–58
cities, dog-friendly, 88
coats, 12–13, 22–23, 71
cognitive dysfunction syndrome (CDS),
  107
colors, 11, 22–23
  See also physical characteristics
conformation dog shows, 93–94, 95
  See also dog shows
contract, sales, 58
costs, 13–15, 28–29, 35, 42
  See also ownership, dog
crating, 54–56, 78

day care, doggy, 27, 88
death, 110–111
dental care, 21, 73–74
  See also health
detection dogs, 92
  See also service dogs
diabetes, 106, 109
diseases, 61–62, 106–109
distemper, 61–62
dog shows, 19–20, 33–34, 38, 57, 93–96
  Agility dog sports, 99–100
  Field trials, 22, 96–97
  Flyball, 100
  Freestyle, 101

Hunt tests, 97–99
dysplasia, 29, 46, 48, 58, 64, 83

ears, 21, 73
elbow dysplasia. *See* dysplasia
England, 18
Europe, 16–17, 18
euthanasia, 110–111
exercise, 12, 35, 82–83, 88, 100, 109–110
eyes, 21–22, 73, 107–108

Fairmont Copley Plaza Hotel, 87
fear-impression period, 67–68
feeding schedules, 66–67
    See also nutrition
field trials, 22, 96–97
    See also dog shows
first aid supplies, 80
fleas, 14
Flyball, 100
    See also dog shows
food. *See* nutrition
foxtails, 81–82
Freestyle, 101
    See also dog shows
Frisbee, 100–101

gender differences, 20, 27, 33, 35–38
genetic defects, 46, 49
    See also health
giardia, 62
grooming, 12, 71–73, 94
    and foxtails, 81–82
growth rate, 77–78

hazards, 52–54
health, 100
    and dental care, 21, 73–74
    diseases, 61–62, 106–109
    genetic defects, 46, 48
    parasites, 14, 60, 70, 79
    puppy, 59–67
    and senior dogs, 104–110
    spaying and neutering, 15, 26–28

vaccinations, 15, 40, 60–63, 78–79
and veterinary care, 13–15, 47–49,
    59–60, 78–81, 105
hearing and vision loss, 107–108
heartworms, 14, 79
    See also parasites
hip dysplasia, 29, 46, 48, 58, 64, 83
Home (Earl), 18
home puppy-proofing, 50–56
    See also puppies
housetraining, 54–55, 74–76
    See also training
Hunt tests, 97–99
    See also dog shows
hunting and retrieving, 9–10, 16–17, 19, 44,
    96–99
hypothyroidism, 108

identification, 25–26, 29
    See also ownership, dog
immunization. *See* vaccinations
indefinite listing privilege (ILP), 98
    See also dog shows
inherited diseases. *See* genetic defects
insurance, pet, 28–29
    See also costs
International Disc Dog Handlers
    Association, 102

Kennel Club of the United Kingdom, 9, 21,
    38
kennel cough (bordetella), 62
kennels (boarding), 88–89
kidney disease, 108–109

Labrador, Canada, 16–17
Labrador Retriever Club (LRC), 17, 23, 38
Labrador Retrievers
    breed history, 16–19, 21, 23
    breed standards, 19–23, 93
    and children, 70, 111
    choosing of, as pets, 32–47
    environment for, 11–13
    and exercise, 12, 35, 82–83, 88, 100,

109–110
and gender differences, 20, 27, 33,
    35–38
genetic defects, 46, 48
grooming, 12, 71–73, 81–82, 94
growth rate, 77–78
hunting and retrieving, 9–10, 16–17, 19,
    44, 96–99
life expectancy, 10, 104
physical characteristics, 10–13, 19–23,
    33
popularity of, 9–10, 17–19
as puppies, 34–35, 41–44, 50–69, 70–76
as senior dogs, 104–111
as service dogs, 9, 90–93
size, 10–11, 20
and socialization, 31, 41, 60, 70–71, 84
temperament, 10–11, 18–19
traveling with, 85–87
See also health; ownership, dog
laryngeal paralysis (LP), 108
legal issues, 28, 29–31
    See also ownership, dog
leptospirosis, 62
licensing, 29
life expectancy, 10, 104
Lyme disease, 62

Malmesbury (Earl), 18
manners, 76
microchips, 26, 29
    See also identification

nail care, 72–73, 81
    See also grooming
National Association for Search and
    Rescue, 91–92
National Association of Professional Pet
    Sitters, 89
National Dog Registry, 26
neutering, 15, 26–28
Newfoundland, Canada, 16–17, 18
Newfoundland Sheep Protection Act, 18
nose, 20–21

nucleus sclerosis, 107
nuisance laws, 30
    See also legal issues
nutrition, 14, 78, 83, 94
    for puppies, 62–66
    for senior dogs, 109

Obedience competitions, 94–96
    See also dog shows
obedience training, 15, 69, 84–85
    See also training
Orthopedic Foundation for Animals (OFA)
    certification, 57, 58
    See also breeders
osteochondrosis, 83
ownership, dog, 24–28
    choosing your Labrador, 32–47
    costs, 13–15, 28–29, 35, 42
    and identification, 25–26, 29
    and legal issues, 28, 29–31
    licensing, 29
    and pet insurance, 28–29

parasites, 14, 60, 70, 79
parvovirus, 61
pedigree, 58
    See also registration
PennHIP certification, 57
pet sitters, 34–35, 87–88, 89
physical characteristics, 10–13, 19–23, 33
plants, poisonous, 52–53
police dogs, 92
    See also service dogs
popularity, 9–10, 17–19
Portuguese mastiffs, 16–17
potty training. See housetraining
progressive retinal atrophy (PRA), 46
puppies, 34–35, 41–44
    caring for, 56–67, 70–74
    and the fear-impression period, 67–68
    grooming, 71–74
    and home puppy-proofing, 50–56
    and nutrition, 62–67
    training, 68–69, 74–76

See also Labrador Retrievers
Puppy Aptitude Test (PAT), 43

Quarantine Act, 18

rabies, 15, 61, 62
raw food diet, 65
    See also nutrition
registration, 57–58
    See also American Kennel Club (AKC)
rescue organizations, 42, 44–46
Retrieval Proficiency Test (RPT), 102
retrieving, 9–10, 16–17, 19, 44, 96–99

Scott, John (Lord), 18
search-and-rescue (SAR) dogs, 91–92
    See also service dogs
senior dogs, 104–110
    and death, 110–111
    See also Labrador Retrievers
service dogs, 9, 90–93
shedding, 12–13, 71
"silver Labs." *See* colors
size, 10–11, 20
socialization, 31, 41, 60, 70–71, 84
spaying, 15, 26–28, 37
specialty shows. *See* Conformation dog
    shows
St. Hubert hound, 16
St. John's dogs, 18, 23
structure, 20
supplies, 14–15, 54, 80

tail, 22
tattoos, 26, 29
    See also identification
teeth, 21, 73
temperament, 10–11, 18–19
theft, dog, 26
therapy dogs, 92–93
    See also service dogs
titles, 40, 94, 95, 96, 98
    See also American Kennel Club (AKC)
Tracking competitions, 96
    See also dog shows
training, 12, 15, 34–35, 68–69, 84–85
    for dog shows, 94
    housetraining, 54–55, 74–76
    and manners, 76
traveling, 85–87
    See also boarding

vaccinations, 15, 40, 60–63, 78–79
veterinary care, 13–15, 47–49, 59–61, 78–81,
    105
vision and hearing loss, 107–108
Volhard, Jack and Wendy, 43
Volhard Puppy Aptitude Test (PAT), 43

Westminster Kennel Club dog show, 95
    See also dog shows
Wind-Morgan certification, 57
World War II, 17, 92

Contributors

SANDRA BOLAN is an award-winning journalist and photographer whose articles on dogs have appeared in such magazines as *Animal Fair*, *Animal News*, *Canadian Pets and Animals*, *Dog Sport Magazine*, *Modern Dog*, *Pets Magazine*, and *Dogs, Dogs, Dogs!* In 2005 the Dog Writers Association of America nominated Sandra for a Maxwell Award, and in 2005 Sandra's first book, *Dogs and Dads*, received an Honorable Mention from the Independent Book Publishers Association. Her other books include *Moms and Paws* (Fetch it Up, 2007). Sandra's dog photographs have been featured on greeting cards and in numerous magazines. When she's not behind a camera or writing, Sandra is a certified professional dog trainer.

Senior Consulting Editor **GARY KORSGAARD, DVM,** has had a long and distinguished career in veterinary medicine. After graduating from The Ohio State University's College of Veterinary Medicine in 1963, he spent two years as a captain in the Veterinary Corps of the U.S. Army. During that time he attended the Walter Reed Army Institute of Research and became Chief of the Veterinary Division for the Sixth Army Medical Laboratory at the Presidio, San Francisco.

In 1968 Dr. Korsgaard founded the Monte Vista Veterinary Hospital in Concord, California, where he practiced for 32 years as a small animal veterinarian. He is a past president of the Contra Costa Veterinary Association, and was one of the founding members of the Contra Costa Veterinary Emergency Clinic, serving as president and board member of that hospital for nearly 30 years.

Dr. Korsgaard retired in 2000, and currently enjoys golf, hiking, international travel, and spending time with his wife Susan and their three children and four grandchildren.